BANKRUPTCY
Why Your Neighbor Had to File

Attorney
ROBERT V. SCHALLER

PUBLISHED BY FRIESENPRESS
IN CONJUNCTION WITH
NATIONAL BANKRUPTCY ACADEMY, INC.

Copyright © 2013 by Robert V. Schaller
First Edition – September 2013

ISBN
978-1-4602-2787-9 (Hardcover)
978-1-4602-2788-6 (Paperback)
978-1-4602-2789-3 (eBook)

All rights reserved.

No part of this publication may be reproduced in any form, or by any means, electronic or mechanical, including photocopying, recording, or any information browsing, storage, or retrieval system, without permission in writing from the publisher.

Produced by:

FriesenPress

Suite 300 – 852 Fort Street
Victoria, BC, Canada V8W 1H8

www.friesenpress.com

Distributed to the trade by The Ingram Book Company

TABLE OF CONTENTS

BANKRUPTCY: Why Your Neighbor Had to File	v
ACKNOWLEDGEMENTS	vii
FOREWORD	ix
REASON NO. 1	1
SUFFERING A MEDICAL CATASTROPHE	1
REASON NO. 2	7
COPING WITH UNEMPLOYMENT	7
REASON NO. 3	15
PAYING FOR COLLEGE	15
REASON NO. 4	25
GETTING DIVORCED	25
REASON NO. 5	39
CONSUMING WITH CREDIT CARDS	39
REASON NO. 6	51
FUNDING A GROWN CHILD'S DREAMS	51
REASON NO. 7	61
FLIPPING REAL ESTATE FOR FUN AND PROFIT	61
REASON NO. 8	69
BUYING A BUSINESS FRANCHISE	69
REASON NO. 9	79
FAILING TO FEAR DEBT	79
REASON NO. 10	85
SELF-LAWYERING	85
ABOUT THE AUTHOR	95

BANKRUPTCY:
Why Your Neighbor Had to File

By: Robert V. Schaller, Copyright ©2012.

For more information about the author, visit:
www. SchallerLawFirm.com/Attorney/Robert_Schaller.html

All Rights Reserved. No part of this book may be reproduced or transmitted in any form or by any means, electronic or mechanical, including photocopying, recording or by any information storage and retrieval system, without written permission from the author, except for the inclusion of brief quotations in a review. If you would like to use material from the book prior written permission must be obtained by contacting the author at Schaller@ SchallerLawFirm.com. Thank you for the support of the author's intellectual property rights.

ACKNOWLEDGEMENTS

I cannot express deep enough thanks and gratitude to my mother Dolores Schaller, who has always provided steadfast love, encouragement, and devotion to me and all her seven children and eighteen grandchildren. My love, admiration, and respect is posthumously given to my father George Schaller, a former judge of Illinois' Circuit Court of Cook County, who stood in my life as a tower of strength and a beacon of wisdom.

My older brother Bill, a partner at the international law firm of Baker & McKenzie LLP, has served as a guiding light in my professional life and a source of pride and cherished friendship in my personal life. Bill is a lawyer's lawyer and a brother's brother. My sisters Gail, Joyce, and Gloria have cheered for me all my life and have showered me with more love than anyone deserves. No brother could ask for more.

I rush to thank my beautiful daughters Katie and Beth for their love, laughter, affection, and devotion. They are God's gift to me here on Earth and make my heart sing. No father could be prouder or more loved than me.

Finally, I thank my wife Nancy for sharing her life with me these past twenty-five years. She has listened to me grapple with my daily struggles as I pass through life pushing King Sisyphus' immense boulder up the hill, one day at a time. I only wish I could give to her as much happiness as she has given to me.

Robert Schaller, 2012

FOREWORD

"Neither a borrower nor a lender be; For loan oft loses both itself and friend, And borrowing dulls the edge of husbandry." William Shakespeare, <u>Hamlet</u>, Act 1, Scene 3. Shakespeare's sage advice, spoken from the lips of Polonius in *Hamlet*, warns of financial danger when debt supplants domestic thrift. This warning was ignored by almost thirty-two million Americans who filed bankruptcy since the 1980s.

Could YOU be forced to file bankruptcy? Eight to ten million more Americans are expected to file bankruptcy during the next five years. Most are currently unaware that the seeds of their financial destruction have already been sown. It is only a matter of time before their massive debt loads become unmanageable and an unexpected shock thrusts them over the edge.

The debt reaper is waiting just around the corner and these Americans cannot recognize him. Read on to determine whether YOU have sown your own seeds of financial destruction by engaging in seemingly benign conduct that comprises any of the Top 10 Reasons that caused your neighbors to file bankruptcy.

Bankruptcy in the modern era respects no income boundaries and attacks all income brackets: affluent, middle-income, and working-poor. Bankruptcy respects no educational boundaries and attacks doctors, lawyers, accountants, engineers, M.B.A.'s, college graduates, and Americans holding high school GEDs. Bankruptcy respects no community boundaries and attacks the inner-city, suburbia, and rural America. Every county in America has felt the impact of the pandemic spread of bankruptcy.

Shakespeare's warning was largely heeded by the Great Depression Generation who feared debt and the resulting garnishments, repossessions, foreclosures and virtual debtor's prison. This Greatest Generation largely shunned bankruptcy relief and those caught in the debt trap infrequently utilized the bankruptcy laws' benefits to shed unmanageable debts because of the social stigma.

This book focuses on a different generation, namely the Baby Boom Generation and its twin troubles: failure to fear debt in the modern era of easy credit; and its willingness to indulge in the immediate gratification of modern-day consumerism. Statistical evidence demonstrates that <u>personal</u> bankruptcy filings in the America increased nearly 350% between 1980 and 2005, while <u>business</u> bankruptcy filings have remained approximately unchanged during the same time frame. See, Thomas A. Garrett, <u>The Rise in Personal Bankruptcies</u>, Federal Reserve Bank of St. Louis Review, January/February 2007.

The dramatic increase in personal bankruptcy filings is easier to comprehend when viewed in real numbers. Approximately two million bankruptcy cases were filed during the six-year period of 1980 to 1985, which equals the zenith of Great Depression Generation filings. In comparison, the Baby Boom Generation filed at a 500% greater rate. Almost ten million bankruptcy cases were filed during the six-year period of 2000 to 2005, which equals the zenith of Baby Boom Generation filings. See, American Bankruptcy Institute, www.abi.org.

This book attempts to correct society's misconceptions regarding the approximate 1.5 million Americans who file bankruptcy annually and to identify what causes these Americans to seek bankruptcy protection. Contrary to popular belief, this subset of Americans is not limited to a narrow socio-economic band on the financial spectrum. In fact, the modern day bankruptcy filer could easily be your neighbor, your doctor, your child's teacher, the guy down the block, the local policeman, the cashier at Target, or a business associate. Most Americans are unaware of the depth and breadth of the bankruptcy pandemic because bankruptcy filers are largely anonymous to the average American. None wears a Hester Prynne-ish scarlet letter "B" on the chest for others to see.

Anecdotally, bankruptcy filers represent a broad spectrum of America, including people whose educational achievement ended with a high school diploma and work at labor-intensive jobs. But college graduates don't escape the bankruptcy net either. Teachers, bankers, and middle-management workers file bankruptcy too. Surprising to some, bankruptcy snags even highly educated professionals, such as doctors, lawyers, engineers, architects, nurses, and computer programmers.

The primary cause for most personal bankruptcies is the amassing of an unsustainable debt load coupled with either a traumatic negative shock to income or an unanticipated spike in expenses. Typical examples of income shocks or expense spikes include divorce, unemployment, and catastrophic medical injuries. But that does not tell the whole story. These are only some of the Top 10 Reasons your neighbors are filing bankruptcy.

This book presents those Top 10 Reasons why your neighbors had to file bankruptcy. Fictional vignettes are offered to demonstrate your neighbors' slide into financial chaos and eventually bankruptcy. Some financial collapses were caused by a single sudden catastrophic event or failed decision, while other collapses were the culmination of a slow, steady slide into debt default.

This book was written to help the tens of millions of adult Americans who have never filed bankruptcy better understand what caused their seemingly normal neighbors to file bankruptcy.

All names, places, characters, and events in this book are entirely fictitious. Any similarity to actual events or persons, living or dead, is coincidental and not intended by the author.

REASON NO. 1
SUFFERING A MEDICAL CATASTROPHE

"Where am I? How did I get here? What happened?" whispered Roy perplexingly in a barely audible voice that spilled out of the mouth of this physically frail man. "You're lucky to be alive," responded Nurse Emily with a broad smile and reassuring face. "Most folks don't survive all you've been through this week," she said. "This week!?! What day is it anyway? How long have I been here?" mumbled Roy.

Roy didn't feel lucky at that moment. His body radiated with pain, emanating from his head and spreading throughout Roy's entire body. He knew he had undergone surgery from the throbbing pain in his skull and the bandages covering his head. But he had to agree with Nurse Emily: he was alive. Confused as to what happened, but alive.

"Just you relax," said Nurse Emily. "I'll tell your family you are conscious," she said. "Your wife's been in the intensive care waiting room with your daughter for days," said Nurse Emily reassuringly with her signature broad smile as she left Room 301 of the intensive care unit at Christ the King Hospital.

Roy strained to remember what had happened. He recalled sitting in an intimate twelve-table Mediterranean-style restaurant called Louigi's Little Italy in Rancho Mirage, CA. Joining him was his wife Susan and his best friend from high school named Bill, who he hoped would help Roy find a job after twelve months of unemployment. But Roy had no recollection after that.

Roy fought to remember what happened at Louigi's Little Italy as he stared at the hospital room ceiling; but he could not. He found it hard to keep focus, especially as his eyes wandered around the intensive care hospital room. He could not help but focus his gaze on the foreign looking medical machines, monitors, and other diagnostic equipment.

"Good morning, I'm Doctor Russell," said the next person to enter Room 301. "How are you feeling today?" Roy responded that his head hurt a lot. He asked what happened. "You suffered a spontaneous rupturing of a brain aneurysm," advised Dr. Russell. The doctor explained to Roy that a brain or cerebral aneurysm is a cerebrovascular disorder in which weakness in the wall of a cerebral artery or vein causes a localized dilation or ballooning of the blood vessel. In short, the doctor said, a brain aneurysm is an abnormal, balloon-like bulging of the wall of an artery in the brain; the bursting of the aneurysm is what causes the problems and leads to death in many cases. Roy heard what Dr. Russell had said, but he did not fully comprehend. All Roy knew was that he was still alive.

"Am I going to live," Roy asked sheepishly? "That's the plan," said the doctor with a knowing smile that pushed up the sagging facial skin around his mouth that testified to his thirty years of surgical experience. "Forty percent of people who suffer a ruptured brain aneurysm die before the end of surgery," Dr. Russell reported.

"You're one of the lucky ones," he reported as he walked out of the room.

Roy's wife Susan was the next to visit. She had a hesitant smile upon her weary face that simultaneously revealed both exhaustion and exhilaration. She had not slept in more than twenty-four hours and had not slept soundly for more than five days. Susan was taken aback when looking at Roy's shaved head and bandages that covered his nine-inch surgical wound starting just above Roy's right ear and traveling to the top of his head. But her man was alive. Susan did not know whether to cry or kiss Roy. So she did both.

Susan explained that Roy had collapsed face first into a plate of manicotti at Louigi's Little Italy restaurant last Saturday night. Initially Susan thought Roy had been joking, but immediately realized that something awful had happened. Susan frantically dialed 911 and moments later an ambulance swept Roy away and rushed him to the hospital. Roy had been told the rest of the story by Dr. Russell.

The financial reckoning-bell was rung when Susan opened the first hospital bill weeks after Roy was discharged from the hospital. Following closely behind were invoices sent by the surgeon, anesthesiologist, and radiologist. Also included in the flock of invoices were bills from the ambulance service, pharmacy, medical supplies, blood labs, and x-rays. Susan didn't know what to do. Without health insurance, she didn't know how she and Roy could ever pay the bills. So, she hesitated, took a deep breath, and then threw the bills and invoices into the garbage without telling Roy.

Roy had been distracted from financial reality and concentrated almost exclusively on rehabilitation. All of his energy was focused on recovering and returning to normal. It was an uphill battle, but Roy was a fighter and gained ground week after week. Roy didn't think about paying any medical bills or finding another IT job. Roy myopically focused on his health.

Susan intentionally distanced herself from financial reality and tried not to think about the looming financial disaster. The hospital alone cost $82,000. The surgeon required another $10,000. The anesthesiologist and radiologist demanded $6,000 more between them. The ambulance, medical supplies, x-rays, blood tests, and other medical bills would easily be north of $5,000. Finally, rehabilitation and regular checkups had been estimated by the discharge nurse at approximately $7,000.

Thirty days later financial reality slapped Susan again. All the medicals bills combined equaled more than $105,000. She knew they had no money to pay these bills. Susan worked without benefits as an accountant's assistant in the billing department of a small injection-molding plastics company earning take home pay of only $675 every two weeks.

Roy, on the other hand, had been unemployed for more than twelve months at the time of the brain aneurysm rupture. He had been terminated from his information technology job at a major competitor of Wal-Mart. His prior $73,500 annual salary had made it easy to pay the mortgage, car payment, food, clothes and other necessities of life. But Roy and Susan knew that the loss of the $73,500 income could not be offset by Roy's meager unemployment compensation benefits.

Central on Susan's mind was Roy's loss of employer-provided insurance benefits, since Susan's employer offered no insurance coverage. Roy had been fully insured with life, health, and disability insurance while he was employed. Upon termination, Roy exercised his COBRA rights granted to by Congress in the Consolidated Omnibus Budget Reconciliation Act (COBRA), which gives terminated workers and their families the right to continue group health benefits provided by their group health plan for limited periods of time.

Roy agreed to pay the COBRA continuation coverage during the early months following Roy's termination. Then the COBRA coverage became prohibitively expensive after the cost jumped to an amount that exceeded ALL of Susan's monthly take-home pay. So, Roy and Susan were forced to cancel the COBRA coverage and "self-insure" --- gambling that neither would suffer a significant medical expense before Roy could regain employment.

The gamble failed. Roy's inter-cranial brain aneurysm ruptured a few months after the COBRA coverage had been cancelled. Consequently, they had no insurance protection and would be forced to pay the $105,000 medical costs out of their own pocket.

Susan knew that the family's combined savings and checking accounts balance was less than $800. Susan instinctively knew that they would not have the ability to save $105,000 plus the inevitable late fees, interest, costs, and attorney's fees for years to come… if ever. So Susan decided not to bother Roy and quietly collected the hospital, doctor, and other medical bills. She stored them in a shoe box hidden on the far left-side of a closet shelf in the unused fourth bedroom.

Denial was no longer possible. Roy opened the door one Thursday morning and was confronted by a deputy sheriff with the Riverside County Sherriff's Office who was there to serve Roy with a court summons and complaint filed by Christ the King Hospital. The hospital was seeking a judgment in excess of $80,000 plus costs. A judge of the Circuit Court of Riverside County had commanded Roy to fully comply with the summons and to attend a court hearing thirty days thereafter.

Roy showed Susan the summons and complaint. Susan confessed and showed Roy the shoe box that now was jammed with duplicative invoices and bills that had been hidden on the closet shelf. Together they realized their financial position was untenable and they needed legal help. They needed bankruptcy help.

Roy Googled "bankruptcy attorney" on his home computer and was directed to the National Bankruptcy Academy's www.NBAlaw.org website as the top link. A review of the academy's website provided extensive information on Chapter 7 bankruptcy basics. The website also provided a free attorney referral program that referred a bankruptcy attorney located near Roy's Rancho Mirage, CA home.

The bankruptcy attorney informed both Roy and Susan of their bankruptcy options, including the right to file a Chapter 7 bankruptcy petition. The Chapter 7 case would result in all of the medical bills being eliminated or "discharged" and the creditors being permanently enjoined from any efforts to collect the medical debts, including phone calls, letters, lawsuits, and garnishments. Roy and Susan accepted the bankruptcy attorney's advice and filed Chapter 7. Now their medical debts have been 100% eliminated and they enjoy a debt-free fresh start in life.

REASON NO. 2
COPING WITH UNEMPLOYMENT

Vito was no angel. He had not held up his end of the bargain. And he knew it. Vito didn't need anyone to remind him. Vito knew it was a man's duty in life to provide financial security for his family, and to protect them from the forces of darkness. And Vito had failed. Not from the lack of effort. But nonetheless he had failed.

But it was not always that way. Vito was a native of the Bloomfield neighborhood in Pittsburgh. He was raised in a happy union family. At twenty-one years of age Vito proudly joined the United Steelworkers union, whose 705,000 man membership made it the largest industrial labor union in North America. Vito worked with girders and columns that provided the structural framework for buildings and office towers being built in and around Pittsburg.

Life was good for Vito during his twenties. He successfully completed an apprenticeship and other formal training that complemented his high school diploma. Work was steady and the pay was good, especially when Vito received overtime. He married his high school sweetheart Maria, who gave birth to two sons and a daughter. Vito bought a modest home in Bloomfield with monthly mortgage payments of $1,465 for thirty years. He and Maria reared the children the best they could and educated them at the local schools. The family regularly attended the parish church.

Vito's financial life started to unravel during his mid to late thirties. Work had been sporadic for a few years. Like a financial yoyo, Vito was flush with cash when he was working, but struggled when he was laid off. Being laid off became more and more a frequent occurrence. He had to tighten his financial belt during those years to make ends meet. Gone were the days of Disneyland vacations and expensive electronic gadgets for the kids. His fishing boat and bowling league were gone too.

Vito had always maintained good credit and a high FICO score by making his mortgage payments on a timely basis. His vehicle payments were consistently made on or before the due date each month come hell or high water. Utilities, phone, and cable were all paid timely.

Credit cards were the "liquidity factor" that kept Vito afloat during rough patches. Vito relied upon "cash advances" from the credit cards to generate the cash necessary to pay merchants that did not accept credit cards. One such creditor was the truck lender to whom Vito had to pay $685 monthly to avoid repossession of his Chevy Silverado 2500 HD. These cash advances carried 28% interest charges that Vito had to endure as the cost of keeping his Silverado.

Vito was lucky that the other vehicle lender accepted credit card payments for the $412 monthly payment on his wife's 2008 Ford Fusion. The interest rate was lower but still added to the burgeoning debt. Other credit card purchases were made for food, clothes, utilities, phones, medicine, newspapers, coffee, donuts, toiletries, and other necessities of life.

When times were good, Vito paid down the credit card balances the best he could. When times were tough, Vito paid only the minimum credit card payment required. During his late thirties, Vito had to rely more and more on credit cards to make ends meet because work became harder and harder to obtain.

By thirty-nine years of age, Vito's credit card balances had crept up to an aggregate amount of all cards exceeding $19,600. Interest rate charges of 18% to 22% on the unpaid balances made the balances all the more unmanageable.

Vito's life changed for the worse the last time he was laid off. Try as he might, he could not find another job. His fellow USW brothers were also without work. It was not a temporary period of unemployment like in the past. This time the it would be a long wait.

Nevertheless, he faithfully followed union rules and did what was asked in efforts to get selected for the next job. But the steel industry was being hurt by the "Great Recession," as some economists and political pundits had labeled it. New construction requiring steel workers was anemic.

Unemployment compensation was putting food on the table and providing for some necessities. However, unemployment was insufficient to pay the mortgage or vehicle payments long term. Vito relied more heavily on credit card purchases to keep his family together in the only home his children had known.

At one point Vito's unemployment benefits were set to expire. Thankfully, this lifeline was not severed because Congress passed an emergency extension of federal benefits that supplemented state benefits that were set to terminate after just twenty-six weeks of unemployment. Vito knew the extension would guarantee continued food on the table and the utilities paid for awhile longer, but he worried about losing the home to foreclosure and the vehicles to repossession.

An Allegheny County deputy sheriff knocked on his door one Thursday afternoon during Vito's forty-first week of unemployment. The deputy served him with a Summons and Foreclosure Complaint in which the mortgage lender alleged Vito was in default with his mortgage note because of four missed mortgage payments. The complaint also sought a court order to evict Vito and his family after Vito's home was foreclosed. Vito knew he had fallen behind on his mortgage payments, but he just did not have the money to pay the lender. He had the heart to pay the mortgage lender, just not the financial wherewithal.

Vito's cars were safer from repossession than his home was from foreclosure. Vito had managed to keep both vehicle loans current by taking cash advances against his credit card and extending his credit card balances to past $25,000. Vito's credit card providers still had not begun to pressure him because he continued to make the minimum payments required on each of his cards.

Vito talked to one of his USW brothers about his financial situation. To Vito's surprise, this fellow union member had suffered through the same experience in the prior year. Vito was urged to contact a bankruptcy attorney to review his options.

Vito contacted a bankruptcy attorney who practiced law in the Golden Triangle of downtown Pittsburgh near the confluence of the Allegheny River and the Monongahela River. The attorney recommended that Vito make a budget and start analyzing his monthly expenditures as a first step towards bankruptcy and financial freedom.

For the next two months Vito kept a journal of all expenditures made in cash and via credit cards. At the end of each month Vito and his attorney categorized the expenses into meaningful statistics. Vito had thought he had pared his expenditures to the bone. But to Vito's amazement, he discovered he and his wife Maria were paying substantially more money each month that he had realized towards non-essential items, including $95 for Starbucks coffee and donuts; $184 for cigarettes; $147 for cell phones; $85 for cable TV; $65 for animal training; $32 for nail salons; $97 for fast food and seated restaurants; $42 for tools; $58 for gifts or parties; $23 for hunting; $87 for non-essential clothes; and $95 for beer, wine and pizza. These expenditures also did not include what Vito called "one-time-only" expenses relating to the almost monthly "special events" like the New Year, Super Bowl, Valentine's Day, Easter, Memorial Day, wedding anniversary, 4th of July, Labor Day, kids' birthdays, Halloween, Thanksgiving, and of course Christmas.

The bankruptcy lawyer tried to refocus Vito's expenditures into two categories: needs and wants. The lawyer urged Vito to spend only on true needs for the next two years in an effort to break Vito's bad spending habits and to replace those spending habits with long-term sustainable behavior. The lawyer had a simple rule of thumb for the consumption of non-essential purchases, "If you didn't NEED the item you are about to purchase when you were a child, then you don't NEED it now." He further implored, "Vito, you need reasonably priced food, clothing, shelter, gas, transportation, utilities, and medicine. But stop buying Starbucks, cigarettes, cell phones, cable TV, fast food, and all the Hallmark created celebrations."

Vito accepted the attorney's advice and worked even harder to curb unnecessary consumption. But Vito's current problem was unemployment and not overspending. It was too late for that. A job and increased income was the key to turning around his life.

Without the income foreclosure, repossession, and bankruptcy were his future.

Vito continued to rely heavily on his credit cards to live the best he could during his extended unemployment. Food, clothes, transportation, utilities, medicine, gas, and other necessities of life gobbled more and more of the "available balances" on his credit cards. He had reached his maximum credit allowed on several of his cards. Vito's combined credit card debt load had exploded past $64,000.

Vito was powerless to stop the foreclosure without employment. He tried refinancing his mortgage, but was repeatedly rejected because of the lack of income. Vito approached his mortgage lender about a loan modification, but could not convince the lender to offer a trial modification. Selling his home would not work either because he was suffering from negative equity, since the value of his home was lower than the mortgage balance owed to the mortgage lender.

Vito felt powerless when his home for over fifteen years was foreclosed and sold by the Allegheny County Sheriff at a public auction. He knew friends from church and other acquaintances whose homes had been foreclosed. But Vito never thought he and his family would suffer the same humiliation. The bank had sold his home with a sale price that was $45,800 less than the amount Vito owed on the mortgage. The lender was now demanding that Vito pay that "deficiency" in full.

Vito and his family were forced to move into a modest apartment. His parents paid the two months deposit. Vito rented a self-storage unit for the larger household items that could not fit into the apartment. Their five-year-old brown and white pet beagle had to given to the animal shelter because the landlord rejected pets.

The final blow landed about twenty-one days later after the eviction. One Tuesday morning he dressed to go job hunting at the local union hall. He kissed is wife good-bye, closed the apartment door, and walked through the snow and the bitter cold towards the apartment complex's parking lot. To his chagrin, he discovered that his Chevy Silverado 2500 HD had been repossessed in the middle of the night. He could not stand the humiliation any further.

He immediately returned to his apartment and contacted the bankruptcy attorney and made an appointment for that afternoon. He pleaded his case to his parents who agreed to pay the attorney's legal fee. The parents had previously refused his request for mortgage assistance because the parents refused to throw good money down the mortgage hole by endlessly paying Vito's mortgage. But now the parents did not object to paying the bankruptcy fee because it was a one-time payment that would automatically grant Vito and his family a debt-free fresh start in life.

Vito filed a bankruptcy case seeking protection under Chapter 7 of the US Bankruptcy Code. He received the automatic protection of a bankruptcy "stay" or injunction that required all creditors to stop any and all collection actions against him. About ninety days later, the bankruptcy court issued a bankruptcy injunction order that protected Vito against creditors to whom he had owed money. These creditors were permanently enjoined from contacting Vito for the rest of Vito's life.

Bankruptcy also eliminated Vito's $45,800 foreclosure related debt deficiency. Erased was Vito's $17,350 deficiency debt relating to his repossessed Chevy Silverado 2500. Most importantly, Vito eliminated 100% of the $67,500 combined debt owed to all of the credit card companies. In total, Vito had discharged over $130,000 in debts. Vito could now focus on finding that next job with the satisfaction knowing that he was indeed debt-free and enjoying a fresh start in life.

REASON NO. 3
PAYING FOR COLLEGE

UCLA was the first of the top-tier universities to accept Lance. Michigan was a close second, followed by Boston College, and then the University of Illinois. But Harvard, Princeton, and Brown sent rejection letters a few weeks later. Lance and his parents were crushed. They were not used to anybody rejecting Lance academically. Accepting UCLA's offer had to wait since there was one last school remaining: Yale.

The envelope finally arrived after weeks of waiting. The return address was Yale University, Office of Undergraduate Admissions, 38 Hillhouse Avenue, New Haven, CT 6511. Lance's mother was the first to spy the envelope after retrieving the mail from the mailbox at the end of her driveway. She called her husband with the news. Lance would learn of Yale's decision after he returned from high school that day. In the meantime, Lance's mother held the unopened envelope hard against the 100 watt recessed ceiling

15

can in the kitchen hoping to get an early glimpse of Yale's message. But no luck.

Lance ripped open the letter as soon as he arrived home from high school. From his shouts of joy his mother knew immediately that Yale had accepted her son. The celebration began! Lance's mother hugged her boy and in her heart knew that all of the hard work and sacrifices made by her son and both parents had been worth it. Lance had landed the prize.

But this story began long before Yale's decision to accept Lance. James and Lisa were proud parents of their son, a high achieving and academically superb student. Both parents had gone to college and then graduate school. James was a successful businessman with an MBA from the University of Chicago. Lisa earned a master of fine arts from Northwestern University, and stayed home to nurture Lance's academic development since birth.

They dreamed of sending Lance to Harvard and developed a twenty-year academic plan. They didn't know then that they were actually sowing the seeds of their own financial destruction.

Lance took to academics from the very start. He received straight A's throughout his grade-school and middle school career. Teachers celebrated Lance and were thankful to have a conscientious student like him in their classes to serve as a role model for other students.

High school proved no different. Perfect scores and setting-the-curve became Lance's goal in each of his classes. He made the principal's honor roll every semester, despite challenging himself in advanced placement courses and honors classes in subjects like biology, chemistry, calculus, trigonometry, and US & European History. Lance proved he was not a robot when he received his one and only "B," in honors AP French.

Nevertheless, Lance's grade-point-average was impeccable and put his class-rank at number two. He earned the Illinois State Scholar certification and was a member of the National Honor Society. James and Lisa celebrated their son's achievement when he was named a National Merit Finalist by the National Merit Scholarship Corporation. Like icing on a cake, Lance was named class salutatorian and was selected to deliver the salutatory at the high school commencement ceremony.

James and Lisa were confident that Lance would obtain high ACT and SAT scores since he had always performed superbly on national standardized tests. Lance's parents took nothing for granted and enrolled their son in an institutional test preparation program years before the big exams. Money was no object; a perfect score was the goal. Lance concentrated with laser-like focus on the preparation materials and practiced intensively into the wee hours night after night.

The hard work paid off! Lance received an ACT score of 35 out of 36 and an SAT score of 2280 out of 2400. James and Lisa suspected that colleges like the UCLA, University of Michigan, Boston College, and the University of Illinois would fawn over a candidate like their son Lance. But would the Ivy League schools admit Lance?

Yale's acceptance letter answered that questions once and for all. The celebration had started!

Lance immediately Facebooked all of his friends with the super news. Lisa called James on his cell phone at work to declare a parental victory over the almost insurmountable academic odds of being accepted into the Ivy League. She proffered that Yale only admits 1,300 freshman each year... and Lance would be one of them. Lisa and James realized then that everything they had hoped for, worked hard for, and prayed for had come to fruition. Admission now proved worth the academic toil, sacrifice, long nights, and occasional tears. Their son was going to Yale.

James thanked Lisa for calling and sharing the good news. He promised to come home early from work for a celebratory dinner that night. But as James was riding the commuter train home from the heart of the city, he began to think about the financial ramifications of paying for college.

College tuition can be staggering when combined with university charges for room and board. Yale's tuition was one of the highest. Yale's campus in Connecticut was far from their home in Chicago, so James factored in the cost of Lance's airplane flights to and from school. The obligatory college visits by the proud parents equated to more flights, car rentals, hotel bills, and other expenses. James estimated the college cost at $230,000 for all four years.

James' income was too high for Lance to qualify for any financial aid package at that point. James and Lisa refused to saddle Lance with any long-term student loan debt. They strongly believed it was the parents' duty to provide the best education possible for their child. James thought of it as a parental contract, an implied agreement that the child would perform at his best in return for the parents paying for the education. That is what James and Lisa's parents had done for them; now it was their turn to provide for Lance.

The tuition, room & board, and travel (collectively, "tuition") for the first semester of freshman year was manageable and James sent Yale the first $27,500. The second semester's payment of $27,500 proved harder. James had been down-sized from his upper-middle management job in downtown Chicago. Therefore, this $27,500 tuition payment had to be withdrawn from the household savings account. Nevertheless, James was upbeat and still believed he would find another position in time for Lance's sophomore year.

James was wrong. The job market turned sour and jobs seemed impossible to find. Job interviews were as scarce as a water park in the dessert. Lisa tried to return to the workplace. But Lisa's job search bore no more fruit than James' search. Time was running out.

Lance's freshman year at Yale had drained the family's bank account by $55,000. Now the $29,500 tuition bill had came due for the first semester of sophomore year. James paid part of it from the final balance in the savings. Unemployment compensation was barely enough to cover the food and other necessities of life---certainly not calculated to underwrite the cost of an Ivy League education. So, James decided to incur debt to pay the remainder of the $29,500 tuition bill. James tapped into an existing home equity line of credit that the bank had approved at a time when James had been enjoying a handsome income.

James incurred even more debt to pay the tuition for the second semester of Lance's sophomore year. James utilized the last of the home equity line of credit to pay the additional $29,500 that came due. But James' cash spigot had been turned off by the bank and couldn't be used for junior year. The bank cancelled James' home equity line of credit after James defaulted on the first mortgage loan. Without obtaining that elusive new job, James simply was unable to make timely mortgage payments on either the first mortgage or the home equity loan.

James was embarrassed when he denied Lance's request to study abroad during the summer between his sophomore and junior year. Oblivious to the his parents' financial predicament, Lance pushed his parents hard believing his good grades had "earned" him the right to study the intricacies of the European Union political structure in Brussels, Belgium. James stayed firm, but continued to hide the family's financial condition from his son. James took some inner solace by noting to himself that $114,000 of the anticipated $230,000 had been paid. Only another $116,000 to go.

Junior year begun with Yale demanding another $33,000. James tapped into his 401(k) qualified retirement account. He contacted the plan administrator and sought a "hardship" withdrawal hoping to avoid the large IRS tax penalty for early withdrawal. James received the 401(k) loan and paid Yale the $33,000.

The "bank of 401(k)" paid the second $33,000 installment of Lance's college obligations. But James had exhausted his retirement account by using the funds to pay the $66,000 owed for Lance's junior year. He utilized any remaining 401(k) funds to keep afloat with the car payments, credit card minimums, and life's other necessities. Through three years, James had paid approximately $180,000 in college tuition, fees, travel, room and board, and other college related expenses.

James refused to reveal the financial chaos to his son out of manly pride. James and Lisa still refused to saddle Lance with any long-term student loan debt. They also refused to seek long-term Stafford or Parent Plus loans from the government. James and Lisa were determined to carry their burden through to the finish line.

Lance had no idea catastrophic condition of his parents' financial situation. From Lance's point of view, his parents were financially fit, living in a nice home in a solid, upper-middle class suburban community and were driving relatively new luxury vehicles. Sure, his dad had been struggling to find another job, but Lance remembered that his dad had always provided in the past and had worked without a job interruption all of his twenty one years of life. He believed his dad would land a great job since he was highly educated and a hard worker.

But in fact, senior year was the worst year for James and Lisa. James remained out of work the whole academic year. Lisa tried to start an eBay business selling gently-used wedding dresses and later Christmas ornaments, but made next to nothing in net profits.

James and Lisa had long since stopped paying the first mortgage payments and the home equity loan payments. Both banks had issued notices of default. The first mortgage lender had filed a foreclosure complaint against James and Lisa. It was a bitter morning when the local county sheriff appeared at Lisa's door and served them with a court summons commanding James and Lisa to file an answer and appearance in response to the foreclosure complaint. They were too cash-poor to hire an attorney.

James and Lisa clung to their home because it had been their home for more than fifteen years, and because they had no place else to live. They knew they could not afford the home, but wanted to stave off eviction. James and Lisa reduced expenses the best they could. Lisa surrendered the family's second car, a 2009 silver Volvo, after the car lender threatened to repossess it for loan defaults. They instinctively knew any available money had to be conserved to keep current on James's car loan. James's car payment was $550 monthly for his 2008 BMW, but they both knew they had no other option other than keeping that car. No car dealer would offer James and Lisa a car loan on another vehicle while both were unemployed and their credit reports trumpeting the mortgage defaults, Volvo loan deficiency, and credit card balances. But James needed the car to live in the suburbs and to drive to any interview that may materialize.

James was still without a job when Lance's tuition payment of $33,000 came due for the first semester of senior year. Concomitantly, James began convincing himself that he was being discriminated against because of his age, fifty-five. James and Lisa were living on credit card charges and loan balance transfers. Lisa charged the first $33,000 for tuition, room and board, and books by dividing the charges over multiple credit cards.

"Spreading the pain" was the slogan Lisa employed. But it wasn't a successful strategy. Harassing collection calls from creditors were routine at dinner time. At least one credit card company had filed a lawsuit against Lisa and James alleging breach of contract for their failure to make payments. Other credit card companies were threatening to follow suit.

James and Lisa had exhausted the last of the available cash advances on the credit cards to pay part of the final semester's $33,000 installment on Lance's college education. So James appealed to the generosity of his older brother Tom to pay part of the final installment. The appeal was successful and the older brother generously donated $15,000.

James was able to close the remaining $18,000 tuition gap by obtaining personal loans from a few longtime close friends. James phrased the money plea as a temporary, short-term loan until he got back on his financial feet. Upon receipt of the friends' money, James and Lisa paid the final installment payment on the $230,000 college obligation so Lance could obtain his college degree. Yale's commencement ceremony would be bittersweet.

James' friends knew his promise to repay them was only a wish, merely a dream. They could see through the haze that had been clouding James' judgment. "This was no loan," said the friends. "It's a gift." The friends wanted to help since they had been Lance's childhood pals since he was in the Little League; they also knew a Yale degree would propel Lance down the path to success.

The friends provided the final $18,000 gift with only one condition: James and Lisa must seek the counsel of a skilled bankruptcy attorney to learn their legal options. James met with the attorney and learned that a Chapter 7 bankruptcy case was the best vehicle for obtaining a fresh start in life—debt free! James and Lisa were told that the automatic stay provisions of the US Bankruptcy

Code acted as a congressional injunction temporarily enjoining the mortgage lender from foreclosing on the home and enjoining the credit card company from garnishing any wages and levying bank accounts.

With the help of the bankruptcy attorney, James and Lisa would become debt-free. They were allowed to eliminate both the mortgage debt and home equity debt without paying a penny by surrendering their home to the bank and moving out. That was a blessing since the home was financially underwater now that the fair market value of the home was substantially less than the total combined mortgage balances owned on the first mortgage loan and the home equity loan. The bankruptcy law also allowed James and Lisa to surrender return their Volvo and eliminate any financial obligation owed regarding the loan deficiency.

James and Lisa said good-bye to all of the credit card debts. The credit card lawsuit was enjoined and all debts owed to all credit card lenders were discharged.

On a happy note, James was delighted to learn that he could keep his BMW as long as he could afford to make the regular monthly vehicle payments on a timely basis. The attorney called it "reaffirming the debt;" to James it meant he could keep his BMW.

Plus, James had obtained a job during the ninety days the bankruptcy case was pending. Both James and Lisa were told that their future income would be their money to spend. They vowed to spend James' new salary on an affordable rental home --- large enough for their son to live in after graduation.

REASON NO. 4
GETTING DIVORCED

BAM! The solid oak front door slammed so hard against the door jamb that the adjacent window panes rattled from the vibrations. Cindy slammed that wooden door as hard as she could to make a physical exclamation point as she stormed-out the marital home for the last time as Henry's wife. At that moment Cindy also knew the marriage was over. If only Henry had not said and done such hateful things. But how could the bell be un-rung?

"Barbara's my soul mate and she fills a place in my heart that you can never fill," Henry had shouted at Cindy after confessing to the existence of his not-so-secret girlfriend. What he had said was patently untrue, and now he wished he had not said it. Nevertheless, it had been said. Henry knew that his wife, like most people, had a fragile ego. So he had hurled the insult at Cindy to belittle her, to hurt her.

Barbs thrown during the heat of a martial battle are intended to rip deep into the heart of the other spouse's psyche. Insults are spewed with the intent to locate and puncture the chink in the other spouse's armor that protects their sense of dignity. Cindy's fight with Henry on that dreadful day was no different. Henry wanted to strike at Cindy… to cause pain. And he did.

Cindy had suspected that Henry had been unfaithful for quite some time. But Henry had perfect cover for his misdeeds. Henry was an interstate traveling salesman for a national computer company headquartered in suburban Trenton, NJ. Henry was the senior sales representative for the Midwest region that covered Illinois, Indiana, Michigan, and Wisconsin. His responsibilities included maximizing sales revenues for his ten-person team.

Henry was not new to computer sales. He had been a sales representative for several different computer companies ever since he graduated from Arizona State University nineteen years ago. Computer sales was his career and he enjoyed a comfortable living as a result of it.

Henry was also not new to interstate travel. For the last fifteen years his job schedule required Henry to live in a hotel five days a week. Henry would leave home each Sunday night and fly to the nearest hotel to his Monday appointment. He would then sleep in a hotel Sunday thru Thursday as he made his sales rounds in that territory. Friday afternoon he would return home to spend Friday night and Saturday with Cindy.

Both Henry and Cindy had been active athletes since their marriage. Henry loved playing tennis with Cindy in the mixed-doubles league on Friday nights at their local tennis club. Saturday mornings were devoted to strength training and long-distance running, since both loved participating in 10k races. Saturday night was "date night," with a local high school girl babysitting their two middle-school aged children.

Henry looked forward to his weekend time with Cindy until that fateful day when Cindy's car was rammed by a distracted teenager driving in a Honda Pilot while texting on his iPhone. Cindy suffered a broken collar bone and severe blow to the head that damaged the inner ear's labyrinth near her brain. Cindy's collar bone eventually healed, but Cindy never fully recovered from the inner ear damage to her labyrinth. Her sense of balance was primarily controlled by a maze-like structure in our inner ear called the labyrinth, which is made of bone and soft tissue. At one end of the labyrinth is an intricate system of loops and pouches called the semicircular canals and the otolithic organs, which help maintain balance.

The doctors labeled Cindy's long-term damage as "vestibular balance disorder." This disorder caused Cindy to feel unsteady or dizzy, as if she was moving, spinning, or floating, even when she was standing still or lying down. Consequently, Cindy stopped exercising and all athletic activities. Cindy now leads a mostly sedentary lifestyle focusing on Henry and her two children.

Henry was supportive initially, believing that Cindy's balance disorder would be as temporary as her broken collar bone. In the beginning, Henry asked his neighbor's wife to substitute for Cindy in the mixed doubles league that eventually became unmanageable. Henry continued to prepare for the upcoming 10k race on Saturday mornings. But Saturday "date nights" transformed into low-key backyard barbeques followed by television with the kids and early bed after watching Saturday Night Live. Gone were the days of fast-paced weekend recreation.

Eventually Henry became resentful. Henry tried satisfying his thirst for adventure while he was on the road. Henry's first goal was to attend a baseball game at every Major League Baseball park in Illinois, Indiana, Michigan, and Wisconsin. He added every minor league parks to his goal.

Next, Henry contacted Sports Illustrated and volunteered to write a monthly article critiquing the twelve greatest golf courses in Illinois, Indiana, Michigan, and Wisconsin. He would play each course with a superpass afforded by Sports Illustrated's press credentials. The course pros would welcome him with open arms and lavish him with benefits and freebies hoping that Henry publish positive PR in the next issue of Sports Illustrated. "What a deal!" he once boasted to his subordinate computer sales representatives, "Playing free golf at the greatest golf courses in the Midwest region!"

In reality, the Sports Illustrated arrangement was not such a great deal for Cindy and Henry's children. They began seeing less and less of Henry as he traveled to different golf courses weekend after weekend during the last summer before the divorce. Henry was gone during the week on business and now he was gone most weekends "working" for Sports Illustrated playing golf.

Unbeknownst to Cindy, Henry had developed a traveling buddy who also enjoyed golf, baseball, and Henry himself. Barbara was her name and she was Henry's subordinate sales representative. Barbara reported directly to Henry. Henry was the senior sales representative and had the power to allocate territory to each of the ten sales representatives comprising the Midwest regional sales group.

More and more Henry mapped the sales territories so that his appointments overlapped with Barbara's appointments. They began traveling together, staying in the same hotels, entertaining the same clients, and spending "down-time" together. They shared dinner together during the week on most nights. Barbara was always ready to join Henry on whatever adventure Henry had uncovered.

They worked out together at the hotel exercise room, and swam in the hotel pool. Barbara had a great two-handed backhand shot on the tennis court and easily outran Henry whenever they jogged together. Barbara's nine fewer years of life and petite figure gave her a distinct athletic advantage.

Cindy confronted Henry one Saturday morning when she noticed a $12,000 Visa charge on the monthly statement, a statement that now had a total revolving balance due of $22,346. The creditor was identified as "Blue Majestic Jewelers" in Grand Haven, MI. Cindy knew Henry had not showered her with any jewelry since the oldest child was born.

"What did you buy at Blue Majestic Jewelers? Cindy asked suspiciously. She long suspected that Henry was having an affair. Cindy suspected the adulterer was a co-worker. Cindy understood that Henry had become distant, distracted, and detached.

Cindy also understood that Henry was only going through the motions when he was home; his passion was gone. Henry routinely retreated to the den in the house for long periods of time to play Gears of War on his Xbox 360. Plus, he would recreate on the weekends without Cindy on a regular basis. Henry had been forging a new life for some time.

The $12,000 jewelry purchase was the final straw that broke the camel's back. "Do you still love me?" Cindy asked. "Do you want to be married to me anymore?" she snapped.

Henry stood silently for several awkward minutes while leaning with his left shoulder planted firmly against the kitchen wall while his right hand partially covering his right eye. Henry's fingers slowly messaged his forehead and temple above his right ear.

"Cindy," he finally said. "I never wanted to hurt you." But you have changed. You're not the fun loving girl I married," he continued. "You have changed since the car accident. You never want to do anything anymore," he complained. "You're always rejecting my fun ideas claiming your disorder prevents you from leaving the house," he said.

Cindy wasn't buying what Henry was selling. "You've been cheating on me with another woman, haven't you?" questioned Cindy. "It's that saleslady you work with, isn't it?" interrogated Cindy. "Admit it!"

Henry couldn't conceal it any longer. "Yes," he confessed. "I have found my soul mate. Her name is Barbara and she understands who I am as a person. She makes me feel alive," he tried to explain. Cindy couldn't conjure up any compassion. "You're her boss for goodness sakes," retorted Cindy. Henry responded, "It's not like that. She makes me feel young again."

Cindy lashed out, shrieking "You bastard. You cheater. You liar." Then she probed, "How long have you been having sex with that home-wrecker?" He lashed back, "Don't say that! Barbara is my soul mate and she fills a place in my heart that you never filled." He immediately wished he hadn't made that statement. But it was too late and he couldn't un-ring the bell. Cindy gathered the children and stormed out of the house.

Henry knew divorce was inevitable. That same day he rented an apartment a few miles from the family home. It was a medium size two-bedroom place where he could stash all of his possessions during the divorce proceeding.

Henry also knew that the divorce would be messy and expensive. So Henry dashed to the local bank and withdrew all of the funds in the joint checking and savings accounts, leaving only a few hundred dollars in Cindy's individual account. Henry also withdrew the full amount of the available balance on the home equity line of credit.

Henry was served with divorce papers about three weeks later when the deputy sheriff of Sangamon County knocked on his apartment door late one Friday afternoon. Cindy cited "irreconcilable differences" as the legal grounds for the divorce. She was also seeking alimony, maintenance, property settlement, child support, and full custody of both children. Not surprisingly, Cindy had engaged the most aggressive divorce attorney in the county. He was also the most expensive.

Before Henry could engage a divorce attorney to defend his interest, he was served again with legal papers. This time, the papers read "Emergency Motion for Protective Order." The motion was scheduled for hearing forty-eight hours thereafter before the Honorable Stanley Waldren of the Sangamon County Circuit Court. Henry understood that a protective order is a civil court order issued to prevent acts of family violence. Henry also knew that a protective order was not necessary since he had never harmed or abused his wife or kids. Therefore, Henry had no doubt that Cindy and her attorney were playing legal hard-ball.

Henry engaged his own divorce attorney by paying a $25,000 retainer. His attorney charged $495 per hour while the associate attorneys charged $290 per hour. Henry's divorce attorney estimated that the total attorney fees for his portion of the divorce could exceed $100,000 or more if the proceeding became contentious --- a distinct possibility given the unnecessary protective order request and the reputation of Cindy's divorce attorney. Henry was also warned that he would most likely be liable to pay for his wife's attorney's fees too.

Judge Waldren issued a temporary restraining order at the initial hearing based solely on Cindy's sworn testimony that Henry had been physically violent, including an episode where Henry had allegedly pushed Cindy to the ground during a heated argument. Henry denied the allegations. Nevertheless, the judge issued the temporary restraining order to guarantee the kids' protection. He then scheduled a continued hearing fourteen days later to consider the full merits of Cindy's allegations.

Both Cindy and Henry testified at the full hearing two weeks later. Cindy presented witnesses who testified on her behalf and against Henry. Henry presented witnesses on his behalf. But Henry had the harder row to hoe because he had to prove that something had never happened. Experts were called before the judge to consider the likely future harm to Cindy and the children.

The judge considered all of the evidence and weighed the merits of the allegations. Judge Waldren issued a final order that terminated the temporary restraining order and denied Cindy's request for a permanent restraining order. Henry had won!

Henry's victory was short-lived. It terminated when Henry received his first monthly invoice from his divorce attorney. The legal fees were $13,500 for both the hearing on the temporarily restraining order and the permanent restraining order. The $25,000 retainer had been consumed to $11,500 in the first month.

Henry next filed an answer to the divorce complaint and denied Cindy's requested relief for alimony, maintenance, property division, child support, and sole child custody. Then they prepared for the financial investigation step of the case.

The financial investigation involved discovering and valuing the marital assets that comprised the marital estate. Henry's attorney anticipated a contentious inquiry because Henry had "raided" the bank accounts upon moving out of the marital residence and because Henry had time to stash money in unknown bank accounts in multiple states while carrying on the affair with his mistress Barbara.

Henry's attorney anticipated Cindy fighting over the fair market value of the marital assets and the allocation of debts that were attributable to each party. Cindy would definitely be fighting over who was obligated to pay the $12,000 Visa debt owed to Blue Majestic Jewelers in South Haven, MI. The attorney explained to Henry that he envisioned a long, drawn-out process that included depositions, interrogatories, subpoenas, and CPAs reviewing financial records.

The investigation process took longer than anticipated since Cindy was convinced that Henry had been hiding assets and stashing cash all while he was having the affair. The depositions were bitter and contentious. Expert CPAs could not agree on the value of the marital home or the net present value of Henry's future income steam from his computer job. More than once the judge was called upon to resolve a motion to compel filed by either Henry or Cindy when the discovery process was breaking down.

Henry was required by his attorney to replenish the attorney's retainer with another $25,000 payment. Worse, Cindy's attorney needed a retainer too. So Cindy made a motion before the judge to force Henry to tender cash to Cindy as an advance on her interest in any future property settlement. The judge granted Cindy's request so she would have money to pay her attorney's legal fees. Henry had to sell the only stock he had to pay the $20,000 retainer to Cindy's attorney.

The parties could not reach an agreement regarding the division of marital assets. They also could not resolve issues relating to alimony and maintenance. Cindy was not ready to accept the terms proposed in Henry's draft Marital Settlement Agreement. Month-by-month passed without an agreement being reached.

The judge required both parties' attorneys to appear in court on a monthly basis and advise the judge on the progress of the case. After several hearings, the judge began showing his increasing displeasure with the slow pace of progress at the monthly status hearings.

Child custody and visitation issues were not immune to contentious negotiations. Each spouse was using the children as pawns against the other spouse. Both denied doing so, of course. Cindy filed a motion with the court for an order granting Cindy with temporary custody of the kids and denying Henry any visitation rights. Cindy pointed to Henry's geographic undesirability because he lived out of state five of the seven days each week. The judge granted Cindy temporary custody, but denied Cindy's efforts to deprive Henry of his visitation rights.

The judge ordered both parties to participate in mediation in an effort to resolve the disputed issues. The judge hoped the parties would act more rationally if a neutral third-party arbiter could diffuse the emotion and mediate the contested issues. The judge's hopes were dashed despite the intensive efforts of the mediator. Neither party would budge. They were intractable. Neither party could accept the position of the other spouse.

Neither Henry nor Cindy were acting reasonably, rationally, or logically. Money was no longer the issue. A fair allocation of the marital assets was no longer a consideration. Both took a scorched earth position. Cindy wanted to cause Henry to feel the same level of pain and humiliation that she had felt from Henry's adultery.

Meanwhile, the legal fees had escalated to a point that neither side could afford to continue. But continue they did --- head down, teeth gnashing in frustration. By now, all of the family stock had been sold, the savings account liquidated, and the checking account drained except for the semi-monthly deposits from Henry's payroll via direct deposit. The home equity line of credit had been exhausted.

Cindy had maxed-out all of her available credit on her individual credit cards. She had taken the maximum cash advances. Cindy's attorney had charged the remaining legal fees until the available credit balance was exhausted. Then, the attorneys had put a lien on the marital residence so that they would be paid their legal fees upon the sale of the home.

Henry's situation was none the better. Henry had drained his 401(k) plan by taking two separate hardship loans. Now the 401(k) fund balance had been depleted. The monthly payments obligation to fund the 401(k) loan repayment plans reduced the amount of Henry's available net payroll income that was available to pay future legal fees --- not to mention available to pay rent, food, clothes, utilities, car payments, child support, etc.

Henry had also depleted the IRA money he had set aside from his prior employment. He had originally transferred that money to an IRA from his former employer's 401(k) plan after he switched jobs. The early withdrawal of the IRA money caused Henry to pay a substantial IRS penalty. But Henry had to do it so he could feed the voracious divorce beast that devours legal fee retainers.

Henry's credit cards were tapped-out just like Cindy's cards. But the case was far from over. The parties were required to submit the issues in controversy to the judge at a pretrial conference because they were unable to reach an agreement on almost anything, except prejudgment child support to Cindy. Pretrial conference rules required both attorneys to present their respective positions to the judge. The judge made recommendations for settlement, indicating how the judge may rule on certain issues at trial.

Not surprisingly, neither party accepted the judge's recommendations. So the judge set the matter for trial. The judge's calendar was booked for the next four months, so the parties had to wait for their trial date. The attorneys took advantage of the time in preparing their respective cases.

Trial preparation included interviewing or re-interviewing prospective witnesses, reviewing experts' reports, taking more depositions, and reviewing the discovery materials previously submitted. Trial exhibits were prepared. Occasionally an attempt was made by one party to get the other party to stipulate to a fact.

Both attorneys demanded even more money before the trial begun. Both attorneys submitted legal fee invoices that contained large unpaid account receivables. The former lovers were now deeply in debt.

The trial date came and both sides answered "ready" to the judge's call from the bench. Cindy presented evidence first in her case-in-chief. Cindy's attorney pummeled Henry the best he could, verbally gouging him repeatedly. Pressing, pushing, squeezing Henry was the main thrust of the attorney's attack. Cindy wanted to prove that Henry had hidden money and should be forced to pay enhanced alimony, maintenance, and child support. Cindy was also demanding an outrageous property settlement in light of the marital assets having been consumed by legal fees.

Henry's attorney fought back with ruthless attacks against Cindy financial irresponsibility. He attempted to demonstrate that Cindy was principally motivated by her desire to "punish" Henry by intentionally running up the legal fees in an effort to leave Henry penniless. Henry fought ferociously against Cindy's attempt to obtain sole custody of Henry's children. Although Henry didn't acknowledge that he had spent very little time with his children over the years, Henry instinctively knew that joint custody of the kids would afford Henry an opportunity to continually jab Cindy with custody complaints and be a perpetual thorn in her side.

"Both sides lost perspective," the judge angrily ruled. The judge entered the Judgment for Dissolution of Marriage by basically splitting the matter down the middle. He awarded alimony and maintenance to Cindy in an amount that Cindy thought was too meager and Henry thought too generous. Next, the judge chastised that Cindy and Henry had foolishly fought over trivial issues and unnecessarily inflated the legal fees in the case. Further, the judge ruled that the increased legal fees had essentially absorbed almost all of the equity from the marital estate. The judge awarded one car to each of the parties, and required each party to pay the vehicle loan that secured their respective car.

The judge continued with his ruling, requiring Henry to pay $53,000 of Cindy's unpaid legal fees and to indemnify Cindy against jointly-obligated credit card debts. Next, the judge ordered Henry to pay the mortgage on the marital home and commanded Cindy to sell the home when the last of the children goes to college.

Finally, the judge granted Henry joint custody of the children with visitation rights every third weekend plus one week during the summer. Henry was ordered to pay child support.

Their divorce case was now complete. It would never be called the case of the century. There would be no movies made enshrining the issues for future generations to study. The case reflected an ordinary, typical divorce case between parties who refused to act rationally in an emotionally charged arena.

It was easy for the judge and attorneys to act rationally in the divorce case because that is their job. They are trained to handle the daily stress much like doctors are trained to handle the stress of an emergency room. Henry and Cindy were not so trained.

In essence, neither party had won the divorce trial. The children hadn't won either. The judge was neutral. It was the attorneys who had won as a result of the divorce. The attorneys were robustly compensated for zealously representing their clients as demanded by Henry and Cindy.

The divorce proceedings had financially ruined Henry and Cindy. The total cost vastly exceeded the $100,000 estimate provided by Henry's attorney. But that estimate had been premised upon Henry and Cindy acting rationally. The total legal fees incurred by both Henry and Cindy exceeded $189,000 plus court costs and expert witness charges.

Cindy had nowhere to turn financially other than to bankruptcy for relief. Cindy's combined debt exceeded $100,000 after factoring in attorney's fees, credit card debts, vehicle debts, home equity loans, and family loans. Cindy sought counsel from an experienced Chapter 7 bankruptcy attorney and was soon on her way to a debt-free life. Cindy filed a voluntary bankruptcy petition and automatically received protection from creditors. The $100,000 debt was discharged approximately ninety days later and Cindy is debt-free.

Henry realized he was not as lucky as Cindy after Henry sought bankruptcy advice. Like Cindy, Henry was able to file bankruptcy and eliminate all of his credit card debts. Plus, Henry was able to discharge the debt owed to his divorce attorney. But Henry was denied the right to discharge his obligation to pay the $50,000 to Cindy's divorce attorney as required by the judge's Judgment for Dissolution of Marriage. Henry was also not allowed to eliminate his obligation to pay Cindy's alimony, maintenance, and child support.

REASON NO. 5
CONSUMING WITH CREDIT CARDS

"You're fired! I'm fired. The whole office is fired. Headquarters is closing the whole branch," proclaimed Jimmy's boss --- the managing director of the Chicago branch of a large California-based residential mortgage loan company which specialized in sub-prime residential mortgage loans. Jimmy feigned surprise, but in his heart he knew his branch had been hemorrhaging cash for more than a year because of the plummeting real estate market. Personally, he had failed to meet his sales quota for the past eight months and sales were still heading further south. His only solace had been that other salesmen were performing worse.

He knew hardship was ahead of him. But he felt financially paralyzed because of the life-style he had created for himself and his family over the past couple of years. How could he turn back now? Would his wife divorce him? Would he lose his home? What would his middle school-aged daughter say?

Jimmy wasn't new to financial hardship, but this time it was different. Jimmy had transitioned since high school from an unskilled laborer to a carpenter's apprentice and then to a fully certified union journeyman. The pay had been good when he had union work, but the money always slipped through his fingers. The more he made, the more he spent.

During the "union" years of his life he had managed to get married, become a father to one child, purchase a Chevy Tahoe with $435 monthly payments, and a buy a home in a near western suburb of Chicago with $1,250 monthly payments. Jimmy was happy during the summer months when money was plentiful. But Jimmy argued frequently with his wife over money woes during the winter months when union carpenters were not much in demand.

Jimmy left the union after being laid off one too many times. He left to start his own business as a home remodeler and general contractor. Work was steady at first, but the income was less than what he had become accustomed to as a union worker. After two years, Jimmy's net take-home pay proved to be lower as a G.C. then as a journeyman.

Debt collectors had been hounding Jimmy for unpaid G.C. bills owed to suppliers who had provided essential building materials to Jimmy on credit. Jimmy had used his Visa and MasterCard credit cards to purchase the lumber, drywall, and other costs of construction from building supply stores. Defaulting on the monthly payment obligations caused more than one supplier to file suit against him in the Circuit Court of Cook County, Illinois.

Jimmy had fallen behind on other bills too. The Tahoe payment was frequently fifty days late and the mortgage lender's legal department had served Jimmy more than once with a notice of an "Event of Default" demanding Jimmy cure the sixty-day mortgage default. Jimmy's wife was pressuring him and his twelve-year-old daughter could sense the tension and stress between her parents.

Jimmy believed his luck had finally changed the day he met a mortgage broker who was refinancing the mortgage of the homeowner whose house Jimmy was remodeling. The broker opened Jimmy's eyes to the lucrative mortgage loan sales market with its big fat commissions and an ever increasing stream of business. Jimmy wanted in!

Shortly thereafter, Jimmy met with the managing director of the Chicago branch of the large California mortgage company. The director hired Jimmy on the spot. In fact, seven other people were hired the same week as Jimmy and all received five days of training the following week. No license or college education was required, just a willingness to work hard and a thirst for profit.

Boiler-room sales techniques were emphasized. Sales pitches mastered. Cold-calling scripts perfected. Jimmy was given his own phone and desk located in a sea of approximately ninety other desks arranged neatly in a rectangular grid approximately five feet apart from each other. No doors, no walls, no cubicles between desks, just desk after desk after desk of hard charging salesmen churning the home mortgage loan market.

Jimmy had struck gold! His first twelve months resulted in Jimmy grossing more money than he had ever dreamed of making. His sales commissions exceeded $120,000 and paid off the remaining balance on his Chevy Tahoe. Jimmy cured the mortgage default. Jimmy paid the credit card debts in full. He was completely debt-free, except for his normal monthly mortgage payments.

Jimmy's timing was perfect. He had become a mortgage loan salesman just as the mortgage loan market exploded in the first few years of the 21st Century. Several consecutive years of $175,000-plus sales commissions changed Jimmy's life. He was on top of the mountain. He forgot about his more humble upbringing and the lessons life had taught him as a laborer and union journeyman carpenter. He convinced himself that his new career would last forever.

Like a modern day Jed Clampett, Jimmy loaded up the truck and moved his family to one of Chicago's ritzy North Shore suburban villages located near the western shore of Lake Michigan. He bought a "McMansion" home and signed "80-20" mortgage notes obligating Jimmy to pay $5,650 monthly. The additional $1,983 monthly tax and insurance obligation was not included in the monthly mortgage payment so Jimmy had to create a private escrow account at his local bank so he would have sufficient funds to pay the taxes and insurance when they came due each year.

Jimmy sold the Chevy Tahoe and purchased a BMW 7 Series four-door 745i sedan. He found the $836 monthly payments "reasonable" given his then current income. Jimmy's wife easily shed her lower middle-class roots and purchased a Land Rover Range Rover with a deluxe touring package and monthly payments of $687. She joined the village's Historical Society, Infant Welfare, and local chapter of the Lyric Opera. His wife accepted the invitations to join the charity-ball circuit where they attended posh black-tie events where men dressed in tuxedos and women in evening dresses.

Jimmy was coerced by his newly minted "socialite" wife into joining the local country club, accepting his wife's argument that his daughter should grow-up experiencing the finer things in life. Jimmy initially resisted because he didn't play golf, but ultimately capitulated when he was told that the cost would average only $750-$850 monthly for the luxury that he never had growing up. Jimmy's daughter began attending middle school at a private North Shore academy, and engaged in weekly horseback training at an exclusive private riding club.

BANKRUPTCY: Why Your Neighbor Had to File

Jimmy and his wife bought room after room of new furniture to furnish the McMansion. He let his wife work with a designer to decorate most of the rooms, including the living room, dining room, great room, and bedrooms. But Jimmy took control of the man-cave that his wife referred to as the home theatre. Custom-made reclining chairs, wood paneling, speaker system, and the jumbo screen were all Jimmy's domain. Nothing but the best was purchased.

The couple vacationed three times a year. Marco Island, Florida was their favorite post-Christmas vacation destination because of the white sandy beaches. Spring-break found Jimmy in sunny Palm Desert, California enjoying the desert heat and penetrating sun. Summer vacations were his wife's domain and frequently she engaged a travel agent who coordinated elaborate vacations. Her favorite spot was the eastern coast of the Tyrrhenian Sea near the outskirts of Rome, Italy. Jimmy's wife pretended the Mediterranean Sea was just too crowded for her refined tastes.

During the workweek Jimmy and his wife exercised regularly by taking Pilates courses from a private trainer at an exclusive North Shore fitness club. They treated themselves to a private chef who came to their home each Wednesday evening to create a gastronomical masterpiece just for the family of three. They dined at restaurants three to four days each week since Jimmy's wife no longer liked to cook. Friday night's ritual included dinner with the whole family at a steak house. Saturday was "date-night" at a fancy restaurant of his wife's choosing.

Jimmy was saving hardly any money despite grossing $15,000 each month in commission income. His fixed monthly expenses relating to the McMansion, both luxury vehicles, and country club membership vaporized most of Jimmy's after-tax income. The remaining income was easily dissipated by the family's excessive devotion to immediate gratification. Jimmy relied upon a bevy of Visa, MasterCard, American Express, and Discover Card credit cards to facilitate the purchases, but these debts were typically paid in full each month before the due date. Only the $18,500 balance on the Discover Card was carried from month to month.

One day the underpinnings started to crack that had financially buttressed Jimmy's adoptive and extravagant lifestyle. Jimmy's income was 100% commission-based and his sales volume had dropped precipitously over the last two consecutive fiscal quarters. After half a year of de minimis income, he started to have doubts about his financial capacity.

Jimmy suspected the joy ride was ending long before that fateful day he was fired by the managing director of the Chicago branch of the large California mortgage loan company. Headquarters in Los Angeles had not wanted to lose the small fortune they had invested developing the Chicago satellite office, including costs related to marketing, advertising, overhead, equipment, and salesmen training. So Headquarters kept buoying the salesmen's spirits to minimize the attrition rate by referring to the market downturn as being only temporary.

"Cyclical" was the buzz word used in the mortgage loan business by the company-employed market analysts, implying that the downturn was both predictable and short term. Jimmy accepted the premise and kept hoping the pain would be short lived. Jimmy faithfully attended the monthly in-house forecast meetings where he was told month after month by staff economists not to worry because the real estate market had hit bottom and would be on a steady upward trajectory starting the fiscal quarter after the current fiscal quarter. The economists always found individual statistics to support their optimistic macroeconomic view of the improving market trends.

That magical quarter, however, never materialized as promised by the salaried in-house economists. Instead of improving, the real estate market kept tanking further. The volume of residential home sales continued to decline sharply fiscal quarter after fiscal quarter, resulting in a dearth of mortgage loan applications for new home sales. Similarly, the real estate values were plummeting, which stagnated the mortgage refinance market. Existing home owners simply could no longer qualify for mortgage refinancing because the reduced market values of the houses caused homeowners to fail the "loan-to-value" ratio requirement demanded by the secondary mortgage market. Minimal new home loans and a dormant refinance mortgage market spelled financial disaster for Jimmy.

Jimmy was financially paralyzed. His family had become accustomed to all the trappings of upper-middle class life. He wanted to quit the country club, but his wife resisted predicting the real estate market would improve. Plus, she claimed resigning from the club would embarrass her and reduce her standing among the socialite crowd running the charity-ball circuit. The same rationale was applied to down-sizing the luxury vehicles.

Jimmy eliminated the weekly Chef visit and started eating at home more often. The private trainer was cancelled in exchange for a Bally's Workout membership. Weekend restaurant expenditures were slashed. All vacation excursions were cancelled and his wife resorted to telling her friends that their next European trip had to be postponed because Jimmy was just too busy and couldn't get time off from work. These expense reductions helped, but were not enough to offset the steep income decline.

As for the McMansion, well, nothing could be done to reduce the cost of homeownership. The diminution in real estate home values that caused Jimmy's income to drop also caused the value of Jimmy's McMansion to drop concomitantly. The fair market value of Jimmy's McMansion was now substantially lower than the combined mortgage loan payoff balances on the first and second mortgages. He could no longer afford to pay the mortgages, but he also could not sell the McMansion either.

Jimmy was stuck. He was now deficit spending approximately $8,500 each month. Refinancing the mortgages was off the table. The home equity line of credit secured by the McMansion had long since been cancelled by the local bank because of the reduction in home value in the neighborhood. He could not sell stock because he had spent all of his discretionary income and never bought any mutual funds or individual stocks. He could not liquidate any 401k or IRA account because he never created such accounts, instead preferring to spend any available cash on a lavish lifestyle. Finally, his savings accounts were drained and his checking account was drawn down to a few thousand dollars.

Credit cards became Jimmy's saving grace. Jimmy had previously applied for more than a dozen credit card, including Visa, MasterCard, American Express, and Discover Card. These credit card companies had joyfully extended credit to Jimmy because of his high income and home ownership in a ritzy suburb. The combined available credit exceeded $190,000!

Jimmy remedied his cash flow problems with cash advances and credit card purchases. Cash advances were judiciously spread across ALL of the cards to minimize the debt owed on each card. This strategy also reduced the likelihood than any credit card provider would cancel their credit card. The cash advances were initially used to pay the mortgage and one of the two vehicle payments. Cash advances were also used to pay other current expenses charged by any merchant who would not accept credit card payments.

Jimmy and his wife used credit cards whenever a merchant offered to take credit. Food, clothing, electricity, gasoline, medicine, cells phones, cable TV, internet service, beauty salons, vehicle repairs, school supplies, dentist, newspapers, periodicals, movie theatre tickets, birthday presents, and holiday gifts were all charged to the credit cards. The vehicle lender that accepted credit card payments added a two percent "convenience fee" to the monthly expense, but Jimmy did not complain. Like the cash advances, Jimmy and his wife were careful to spread the credit card pain equally over all of the credit cards.

None of the credit card companies complained. Jimmy's balances were growing rapidly each month, but appeared manageable by the credit card companies' perspective. Jimmy was no longer paying the monthly balances in full by the due date. Instead, Jimmy was utilizing what little money was being generated from mortgage loan commissions to pay the minimum balance required by each credit card. Some credit card companies demanded a $100 minimum payment and other companies demanded more. Jimmy made sure he paid the minimum required on each account.

Jimmy's collective balance exceeded $100,000 after the first year and was still growing. He simply did not know where to turn. "What other job would offer a guy the chance to make $175,000 annually without a license or college degree?" Jimmy kept asking himself. He had no answer.

The loan mortgage market was dead. Other mortgage companies had gone bankrupt. Other branches of out of state mortgage loan companies had closed. Nobody was hiring guys like Jimmy unless they had a book of business.

Jimmy kept praying that the real estate market would hit bottom and rebound sharply so he could start generating big commissions like the good old days. Meanwhile, he continued with the strategy of spreading the credit card charges equally among all the creditors. The minimum payments kept all of the creditors happy. Jimmy was now being charged 18% to 22% interest on balances due and the credit card companies collectively were generating interest income of more than $30,000 annually. "That's the price I have to pay for credit," he said to himself. "At least I have available credit on my credit cards!"

Jimmy's financial world was jolted yet again when he received his first notice from Visa that it had reduced its available credit balance to zero. Visa's written notice gave no specific explanation for the credit reduction, other than citing general adverse market conditions and governmental intervention in the credit market as causing Visa to reduce available credit balances to many customers similarly situated. Jimmy called Visa at the 800 number provided in the notice to complain; but the Visa representative did not budge. The long and short of it, Jimmy would not be allowed to use that Visa card again.

Jimmy continued charging credit cards as the collective $172,000 debt balance neared exhaustion. Jimmy was now in a full panic. The mortgage market remained moribund for the third straight year. He had taken a job at Builders' Square utilizing his union carpentry knowledge, but that provided only food money. He had not paid the house mortgage payment for more than six months and had not paid the real estate taxes for more than a year. Foreclosure proceedings had already been implemented by the first mortgage lender whose almost $700,000 note was secured by Jimmy's McMansion.

All but one of the credit card companies had terminated credit. The remaining card's available balance was less than $2,000. Jimmy had reached the end of his rope.

In desperation, Jimmy contacted his old union boss for some guidance and possible inspiration. "Start over! Get a fresh start in life," said his old boss without hesitation. "I'll refer you to the bankruptcy attorney who helped Tommy McMaster eliminate ALL of his debts. You remember Tommy, don't you? He has never been happier," the boss proclaimed. And that's what the union boss did.

Jimmy contacted the referred bankruptcy attorney and scheduled an appointment. Jimmy didn't realize that bankruptcy relief was available to guys who owned homes valued at mor han $700,000. Plus, he had just assumed bankruptcy was not an option since he previously made more than $150,000.

Jimmy was advised that in exchange for becoming debt-free the US Bankruptcy Code required him to surrender his McMansion, return the BMW, quit the country club, and forego the other upper middle-class trappings that he had embraced the past few years. But the trade-off was easy. Jimmy had already acknowledged to himself long ago that he had lost the ability to maintain those trappings when his job cratered. It had been only a matter of time until he lost physical possession.

The bankruptcy attorney advised Jimmy that the value of his home did not matter for Chapter 7 bankruptcy relief. Similarly, the attorney advised that Jimmy's former income would not prohibit Jimmy from eliminating his mortgage obligations, vehicle obligations and credit card obligations. Bankruptcy indeed would provide the fresh start towards a debt-free life.

At last, Jimmy was debt-free and had been awarded a fresh start in life thanks to the bankruptcy laws. Now it was time to rebuild his life.

REASON NO. 6
FUNDING A GROWN CHILD'S DREAMS

"Are you the Mildred Smith who lives at 324 Sycamore Street?" asked the short, middle-aged policeman wearing the gray Stetson-style hat who had knocked on Mildred's front door. "Yes, and how can I help you this afternoon officer?" answered Mildred after studying the badge on the man's uniform as she stood partially protected behind the oversized oak door. She already knew the answer, but asked reflexively anyway as she looked past the man and focused on the large Burnham County Sheriff's Office decal plastered alongside the police squad car.

"I am a deputy sheriff with the Burnham County Sherriff's Office and I am here to serve you with this court summons and complaint filed by Motor City Mortgage Company," said the officer. A judge of the Circuit Court of Burnham County had commanded Mildred to attend a court hearing and to fully comply with the summons. "I suggest you contact a lawyer ASAP if you want to keep your home," offered the deputy.

Mildred knew she had financial trouble long before the sheriff's deputy knocked on her door. Her financial problem had started about a year before on that dreadful day when her 52-year-old son asked his mother for a substantial loan to start a business. This is her story.

Mildred was a 75-year-old mother of one adult child and the proud grandmother of three adorable grandchildren. She had been married for more than forty years to a wonderful, stable Ford Motor Company factory worker. Together they had lived modestly in a three-bedroom ranch house in a middle-class to lower-middle class neighborhood of Detroit.

All their lives they had lived by a simple financial rule for discretionary purchases: they did not buy anything until they had the cash to pay for it. They deferred gratification and saved their pennies. The only exceptions were a home mortgage and a car loan.

They had no credit card debt. They drove a Ford, of course. They had paid Ford monthly loan payments on a regular and timely basis all their lives. Their current Ford vehicle loan had been paid off after five years of toil.

A "burning of the mortgage" party was hosted by Mildred and her husband to celebrate after the last of the 30-year mortgage payments was made. Financial freedom was finally theirs. It had taken thirty years of living in the same house and making the payments faithfully, but the house was finally theirs… free and clear of all mortgage liens. It was their financial nest egg for their retirement.

Mildred suddenly became a widow one Sunday morning after her husband suffered a fatal heart attack. Since then, she lived modestly on a widow's pension from Ford Motor Company these past ten years. Combined with Social Security payments, Mildred was able to pay for the necessities of life: food, clothes, medicine, gas, utilities, real estate taxes, and gifts for her family at birthdays and holidays. She was blessed with good health for a 75-year-old and she could meet here expenses as long as she remained financially frugal.

One night her only child overturned her economic apple-cart and asked for a large loan. He was a man in his early 50's who had struggled all his life with bad credit. The son worked in a warehouse and was married with three daughters. Mildred soon recognized that he was suffering through a mid-life crisis and wanted more out of life. "I don't want to end up working a factory job all my life like dad," he said.

Instead, Mildred's son wanted to pursue his dream of being a retail merchant near the Ford Motor Company World Headquarters in Dearborn, MI. He had already talked to both a mortgage broker and a real estate broker. He described his dream of opening and operating a picture frame store in the downtown business district of an affluent suburb. The son was sure he could "make his fortune" selling custom picture frames at inflated prices to upper-middle class consumers.

He had already done some research and discovered that framers enjoyed a hefty profit margin because the prices charged to customers vastly exceeded the cost to purchase the frames from distributors. With the real estate broker's help, Mildred's son located an empty storefront to lease in an affluent Detroit suburb just fifteen miles from Mildred's home.

The problem was that the son needed seed money to get started. "Mom, can you loan me some money?" the son asked while having dinner with Mildred. He knew Mildred had limited savings. But the son also understood that Mildred had huge equity in her unencumbered home that could be tapped into by a home equity loan secured by a mortgage on Mildred's home. The mortgage broker had explained the details to the son; the broker's commission would be $3,500 on a $75,000 loan.

The son assured Mildred that she would not have to pay any money on the $75,000 home equity loan. The loan would be in Mildred's name as obligor and mortgagor, but the son assured Mildred that he would pay all the interest and principal payments on the loan out of profits from the future business.

Mildred's instincts and life-long behavior told her to say no to her son's request, avoid debt, and live frugally. However, reluctantly, Mildred agreed because of her love for her son.

The son received the net proceeds from the $75,000 loan transaction with Motor City Mortgage and started his business even though he had no innate business acumen. He had no prior business experience. No background in framing. No retail merchandising or marketing skills. No sales or office experience. In fact, his prior jobs had been limited to working at McDonalds after high school and in an auto parts supplier's warehouse after one year of junior college.

Not surprisingly, the framing business failed the first year. The son had exhausted all of Mildred's home equity loan and spent all the net revenues of the business. Being a businessman proved much more difficult that he had ever imagined. The business closed with nothing being paid on the $75,000 home equity loan but the interest.

Three months after the business closed Mildred received her first demand letter from Motor City Mortgage Company. The letter respectfully reminded Mildred that the home equity loan was seriously delinquent and needed to be paid. Mildred immediately contacted the collection officer whose name appeared at the bottom of the demand letter and explained her situation. The officer appeared to sympathize with the 75-year-old grandmother, but he firmly stated that the mortgage must be paid or Mildred's home would be foreclosed and Mildred evicted.

Fearing eviction, Mildred tearfully appealed to her son to cure the mortgage default by making the mortgage payments on her behalf as promised. The son said he was unable to make the home equity loan payments because he was unemployed. Mildred knew she was in trouble.

Motor City Mortgage mailed the official "Notice of Default" letter to Mildred after the fourth month of no payments. The notice declared that Mildred's loan deficiency would be sent to the lender's legal department for legal action if the mortgage default was not cured within thirty calendar days. Foreclosure and eviction were suggested in a thinly veiled threat.

Again, Mildred called her son seeking help. She was delighted that her son had great news to share. Her son had obtained a job in a warehousing facility of a national brand cookie company. The pay was better than then the pay at his former auto parts warehousing job, with insurance benefits included too. He chuckled to Mildred, "Maybe ending up working a factory job like Dad would not be so bad after all." Life was certainly looking better for the son.

But when it came time for paying any money to Mildred or to Motor City Mortgage, he reneged. "Mom, money is tight right now," he said. "Before I pay any more money related to that stinking business, I have to make sure I pay my own rent and keep food on the table for me and my family," said the son.

"What about me!" shrieked Mildred. "Sorry, Mom, I just can't spare a dime at this time. Maybe next month I can…," he said. In tears, Mildred hung up abruptly.

Subsequent calls over the next few months proved no different. "Money's tight right now, Mom," was always the answer, even though Mildred's loan was taken for the sole benefit of starting her son's business. Long forgotten was the son's mid-life crisis and the son's assurance to Mildred to repay the home equity loan.

The son's commitment to his wife and children may have been admirable, but his abandonment of his mother Mildred was inexcusable. After all, Mildred had been debt-free and living comfortably within her means when the son had requested the loan. Now, Mildred was in jeopardy of losing her home to foreclosure and being evicted.

Needless to say, Mildred was deeply distressed but not surprised the day the Burnham County Sheriff's deputy knocked on her door and served her with a summons and complaint commanding Mildred to appear before Judge William J. Lynch in foreclosure court. In Count I of the complaint, Motor City Mortgage alleged she was in default with her home equity loan obligations. Count II of the complaint further alleged that Mildred had willfully failed to cure the mortgage arrearage after a timely demand had been made by Motor City Mortgage Company. She knew she was guilty as charged.

The summons commanded Mildred to appear in court for a hearing before Judge Lynch. Mildred gathered all of her mortgage documents on the day of the hearing and traveled to the courthouse for the dreaded foreclosure court hearing. She had trepidations since she had never been inside a courthouse. On her way, she telephoned her son with a last gasp of hope that her son would bail her out of trouble. "Sorry Mom, but I wish you luck," was her son's response. "Call me after court and let me know what the judge says," he requested.

Mildred walked up to the courthouse doors and was confronted by the security detail of the Burnham County Sheriff's Office. They were in charge of court security and they took their job very seriously after September 11, 2001. Everyone but the attorneys had to meander through the roped-off holding area waiting to be x-rayed. Bags were inspected; purses were searched. Mildred felt uncomfortable being eyed suspiciously by the sheriff's deputies like a common criminal.

While waiting in line, Mildred noticed that the mortgage lenders' attorneys gained immediate access to the courthouse by waiving a privileged "attorney bar card" which allowed attorneys to bypass the security blockade. Mildred instinctively knew she was at a great disadvantage and a sense of dread started to flood her senses.

She rode the escalator to the second floor and located Courtroom 2008 on the west side of the courthouse after receiving directions from the sheriff's deputy. "JUDGE WILLIAM J. LYNCH" had been chiseled into the over-sized brass nameplate to the left of the massive floor-to-ceiling mahogany double-doors. Mildred checked the courtroom number on the front of the summons to confirm she was at the right courtroom.

Mildred walked trepidatiously into the courtroom and unexpectedly made immediate eye contact with the Honorable William J. Lynch, lord-high chancellor, presiding judge of the chancery division of the Circuit Court of Burnham County. Judge Lynch was seated behind his massive mahogany "bench" that was elevated several feet above the ground. He was hearing legal arguments from a small cadre of mortgage lenders' attorneys standing before him in a pending lawsuit.

To the left of the judge stood the courtroom deputy sheriff, who had a holstered gun and was charged with the singular duty of protecting the judge and enforcing order in the courtroom. The courtroom bailiff was seated to the judge's far left. The courtroom stenographer was seated to the right of the judge and recorded every word spoken by the judge and attorneys.

Mildred wondered why Judge Lynch momentarily paused to notice her enter the crowded courtroom of at least seventy people. Did it had anything to do with her being substantially older than anyone else in the courtroom, even the judge? Mildred sheepishly sat in the back of the courtroom waiting for her case to be called.

"Motor City Mortgage Company versus Mildred Smith of 324 Sycamore Street," proclaimed the judge's bailiff. The lawyer for Motor City Mortgage Company leaped from the counselor's table to the attorney podium stationed before the elevated bench that separated the lawyers from the judge. "Good morning, Your Honor," said the attorney. Mildred took longer to reach the podium since she had been seated in the rear of the courtroom. She reverently said "Good morning Judge Lynch."

Happily, the judge seemed to be protective of Mildred and demanded an explanation from the Motor City Mortgage attorney why they would be attempting to foreclose upon and evict a 75-year-old woman. The attorney held his ground and accused Mildred of failing to pay her home equity loan that was secured by a mortgage lien on her home. The attorney added that Mildred had refused to cure the mortgage default even after the lender had tendered the Notice of Default.

"Is this true Mrs. Smith?" asked the chancery judge. "Yes," she sadly said. Nevertheless, Judge Lynch showed extreme compassion and exercised the court's broad equitable powers granted a chancery judge. "In the interest of justice and due equity," he said, he granted Mildred breathing room by entering and continuing the foreclosure hearing for several months over the lender's attorney's objection.

The court also recommended that Mildred use the time wisely and immediately contact the Burnham County Bar Association for a referral to an experienced bankruptcy attorney who could help save her home. Mildred thanked the judge and promptly fled the courtroom fearing the court may change its mind. She immediately contacted the bar association.

Mildred was delighted when the bankruptcy attorney referred to her explained that she could stop the foreclosure lawsuit and avoid eviction by filing a Chapter 13 bankruptcy petition with the Clerk of the US Bankruptcy Court for the Eastern District of Michigan. The automatic stay provisions of the US Bankruptcy Code would automatically imposed a congressionally mandated injunction upon Motor City Mortgage that would prohibit the continuation of the foreclosure lawsuit and prevent Mildred's eviction.

Furthermore, she was told that the bankruptcy laws could save her home and force Motor City Mortgage to comply with a court-ordered repayment plan that would allow Mildred to repay the mortgage arrearage over sixty months... even if Motor City Mortgage objected and would rather foreclose and evict Mildred.

Mildred took the bankruptcy attorney's advice and saved her home by filing Chapter 13 bankruptcy. She knew she could repay the mortgage default if given five years to do so, bu otor City Mortgage had never offered Mildred that option. Mildred established a repayment plan approved by the bankruptcy court that was within her budget. Although her budget is really tight, she now lives with the peace of mind that her home is saved and she can continue living safely during her senior years.

Mildred's only sadness is the memory of her son running from his duty, shirking his financial obligation, and abandoning Mildred during her time of need.

Mildred also regrets yielding to her maternal instinct to help fund her grown child's dreams and not sticking to the common sense money management principles that she and her husband had lived by all their lives --- If you don't have the cash to pay for something you want now, then don't buy it now. Instead, save your pennies and reconsider buying it later when you have saved enough to afford it!

REASON NO. 7
FLIPPING REAL ESTATE FOR FUN AND PROFIT

Randy was a typical middle-class American who enjoyed the stability of suburban living in Los Angeles. He was married to a darling wife and enjoyed his beautiful children: one each in grade school, middle school, and high school. Randy had a stable job as a commercial plastics salesman and made a comfortable living that supported his family obligations.

Randy was a homeowner with a swing-set in the backyard and two cars in the garage. He had an acceptable monthly mortgage payment and two car payments. But he could manage that responsibility nicely and still have a little money left-over each month to save for an annual family vacation and a small college tuition fund.

Then it happened! Randy was listening to his car radio driving North on I-405 near Santa Monica Boulevard as he was driving between sales calls when he heard Ulysses' tempting sirens' song. It took the form of a radio commercial inviting Randy to a free real estate seminar at the Palomar Hotel on Wilshire Boulevard in Westwood. The commercial offered Randy the opportunity he had always wanted: to become a millionaire, independently wealthy, and have a chance at the "good life."

Randy knew in his heart that his middle-class job would never result in him achieving the good life. Now was his chance. So he attended the free, no-obligation seminar at the Palomar Hotel just blocks away from the Anderson School of Business on the UCLA college campus.

The Palomar Hotel was packed with 150+ dreamers hoping this might be their chance of a lifetime too. The seminar speaker was a smooth-talking motivational speaker. He assured Randy that there were "future" millionaires in the audience. Randy was asked to look around him and attempt to locate the next millionaire. Randy saw people just like himself and he asked himself why couldn't he be that next millionaire. In fact, by the end of the seminar, he started believing he would be the next "chosen one."

The motivational speaker was confident, bold, and assertive. "Millionaires are being minted by my proprietary program," the speaker proclaimed. He presented a PowerPoint presentation that explained how easy it was to make a personal fortune without any specialized training or cash investment obligations. Sound familiar? Similar advertisements air on the radio daily. Something for nothing always has had a good ring to it.

Residential real estate was undervalued all over Los Angeles, Randy was told, and sure to increase in value between 10% and 20% per six month period. The proprietary program would show Randy all the essentials: how to locate the quality properties; how to obtain a mortgage with no money down; how to rent the properties to generate cash flow; how to manage the rental income to service the mortgage debt; and how to flip the properties for huge profit six months down the road.

Randy had heard of other people enjoying huge profits in real estate speculation and thought now was finally his chance to become a millionaire and secure his financial future. The motivational speaker came in for the kill. He flashed written testimonials on the projector screen from unidentified persons going by the first names of Tony, Max, and Mark. Each person claimed to be an alum of the speaker's "program" and each claimed to have made millions of dollars implementing the speaker's program.

The motivational speaker offered to teach Randy and the other attendees how to locate the pot of gold---for a mere $3,000 "program" fee and a percentage of the future profits. A hush came over the room as Randy and the others pondered the $3,000 fee. It sounded steep to Randy, representing several months of savings, and requiring an explanation to his wife.

The speaker anticipated the hesitation over the fee amount. He countered, "the first twenty-five people committing to the program that day would get the motivational speaker as a 'private coach' to help guide them through their first million dollars of profit." Randy's resistance crumbled; he jumped at the chance. He raced for the registration desk; he was twenty-first person in line. He charged the $3,000 to his credit card and his dreams began traveling down the road in search of the good-life.

Randy went home and explained to his wife that he had just been offered a chance of a lifetime. Randy's spouse was skeptical but was swept away with Randy's enthusiasm. The spouse took care of the children and did not work outside of the home. She secretly thought there was a better way to spend the $3,000. But she admitted that she didn't understand real estate speculation, but had heard millions were being made by other people. She just didn't know of anyone in particular.

Randy attended the follow-up training offered by the motivational speaker about two weeks later at a local Holiday Inn. The motivational speaker taught Randy how to target homeowners in foreclosure who had substantial equity in their property. Randy was trained to knock on the door of the home in foreclosure. The speaker warned Randy against appearing to be an investor since targeted homeowners in foreclosure would be defensive.

Instead, Randy was counseled to act as a neighbor who frequently walked by the target's home and accidentally discovered it was in foreclosure. The speaker counseled Randy to offer to help the homeowner keep their home by Randy paying the mortgage default. All the homeowner had to do was transfer title to their home to Randy by executing a quit claim deed. Randy would be nice enough to "rent" back the home to the homeowner as long as the homeowner would continue to make rental payments on a timely basis in an amount equal to the normal future mortgage payments. The small print said that the homeowner would be evicted from the home if the homeowner failed to pay the "rent."

A direct mail campaign was also advised. Randy was given sample direct-mail pieces to send to homeowners in foreclosure who had significant equity. The direct mail pitched Randy as a family man who wanted to buy the target's home because Randy wanted to move into the neighborhood with his wife and kids. Randy was warned never to portray himself as an investor.

Mortgages were another matter. The motivational speaker showed Randy how to obtain no-documentation-loans to purchase the distressed property from people in foreclosure. The training urged Randy to utilize anticipate income on the loan application instead of current income. After all, the trainer stated, the lender is only looking to determine the borrower's ability to make the anticipated mortgage payments.

Randy was also counseled to seek low interest rate owner-occupied financing by asserting he would be living in the property after it is purchased, even though Randy knew that was false. Traditional investment financing would be too expensive and too hard to acquire. Glossing over the fraudulent nature of the loan application, Randy would be able to obtain the necessary mortgage financing to buy his speculative investment properties.

Armed with these weapons, Randy ventured forth to seek out his fortune. Almost immediately, Randy found face-to-face solicitations uncomfortable. Knocking on the doors of a person in foreclosure was not his cup of tea because of the homeowners' deep suspicion of strangers. But Randy found direct mail to be a great way to generate sales leads. Once a homeowner in foreclosure contacted Randy, he used his natural sales skills honed by years of commercial plastics sales experience. Randy was convincing in his pitch that he was doing the homeowner a favor by helping the homeowner out of foreclosure.

Randy quickly purchased his first speculative property in West Hollywood, CA for about $200,000. No-documentation financing for the purchase was easily obtained just like the motivational speaker said it would. Randy was on his way to riches.

Randy found this second home in Santa Monica, CA. A $250,000 purchase financed again by a no-documentation loan. Third, fourth, and fifth properties were quickly purchased in the northwestern, western and southwestern parts of Los Angeles for $275,000, $300,000, and $150,000 respectively. Obtaining no-documentation loans became a breeze for Randy.

The first hint of trouble began when Randy's tenant in the West Hollywood, CA property stopped paying rent and Randy couldn't "flip" the property as fast as he thought he would. He needed the profit from the property to help service the mortgage debt on the remaining properties. The lender was pressuring Randy for mortgage payments; he began to sweat. Randy pressured the realtor to sell the West Hollywood property fast or he would have to engage a different realtor.

Luckily, almost magically, the realtor located a buyer for the West Hollywood property who was willing to pay $325,000. Randy was saved. He paid the realtor, closing costs, and paid off the first no-documentation loan. "The motivational speaker was right," he thought. No harm to the mortgage lender; no foul. Randy kept the remaining $50,000 of profit and used it to service the loan on the remaining four properties.

Spurred on by his successes, Randy again heard the siren song sung by the motivational speaker to invest in allegedly undervalued property in other parts of the United States. The next property was in Florida. After all, everyone loves Florida so it must be great investment opportunity, he thought. Randy bought two condominiums for $125,000 each, properties five and six. No-documentation financing was utilized again.

Thankfully, the Santa Monica, CA property was sold and Randy was again flush with cash profits and able to continue servicing the mortgage debt on the remaining properties. Randy's thirst for the good-life started to get ahead of him. He quit his job to become a full-time real estate speculator.

With the help of the motivational speaker, Randy purchased two more properties in foreclosure in South Carolina for a total of $275,000, two properties in Nevada for a total of $200,000, and another property in California for $350,000. All debts were funded with no-documentation mortgage loans. Randy was now a real estate mogul traveling in the fast lane to financial riches, a true testament to the magic of the motivational speaker's "proprietary program."

Randy though he was rich. He owned ten investment properties across America appraised at over $2,500,000. But Randy's mortgage debt was a whopping $1,800,000. He was not concerned because he had amassed approximately $700,000 in paper profits in less than a year since the first Palomar Hotel seminar. That is more than he could ever have saved in a lifetime as a commercial plastics salesman.

Then the real estate market started to sour. New properties were becoming easier to find, but the equity spread in the properties were getting smaller and smaller. The difference between the fair market value of a targeted property in foreclosure was moving closer and closer to the purchase price. The potential profits were declining.

Randy became more concerned when he sold a Los Angeles property for an amount only slightly greater than the mortgage amount owed on the property. Very little profit was realized. The American economy was souring in tandem with the real estate market.

Randy's tenants began paying rents late or not at all. Randy's adjusted cash flow was totally insufficient to cover Randy's monthly obligations to service the remaining mortgage debts. What rental income came in was quickly expended servicing the mortgage debts.

Mortgage lenders began to call after Randy started defaulting on the monthly mortgage payments. The real estate values had declined so that the fair market values of the properties were now below the amount of their respective mortgage balances. Randy's $700,000 in paper profits had evaporated.

Randy was stuck and had to make a decision. Should he sell the properties for a loss or hold onto the properties by battening down the hatches and weathering the storm? Randy speculated that the real estate market down-turn would be short lived and the fair market value of the properties would return to their former market highs.

Randy's guess turnout out to be folly. The real estate market continued to deteriorate until it finally hit a free-fall in some areas. Randy's dreams were crashing around him. He was helpless and unable to right the sinking ship. Paper profits had vanished quicker than the time it took to amass them. Randy was defenseless as the banks filed foreclosure cases against him one property at a time. Randy had no defense and no money to cure the defaults.

Bank by bank foreclosed on the properties. Randy lost all ten properties. Deficiency judgments were entered against Randy whenever the proceeds garnered from the sale of a property were insufficient to pay the mortgage balance owed on that property. Randy was personally liable to pay the deficiency judgments and the amount totaled into the hundreds of thousands of dollars.

Randy initially ignored the banks' requests to pay the deficiency judgments. His wages began to be garnished after he obtained a new job. Randy sought bankruptcy advice from an experienced attorney to help him discharge his debts.

Randy filed Chapter 7 bankruptcy to eliminate and discharge all of the debts owed to all of the mortgage lenders relating to all of the investment properties. The creditors were blocked from collecting money by the bankruptcy injunction and Randy got a fresh start in life. Randy was now debt-free and vowed never to speculate in real estate again.

REASON NO. 8
BUYING A BUSINESS FRANCHISE

Cindy was a divorced mother living in a Miami suburb who had just celebrated her 50th birthday. She was the mother of two adult children who had kids of their own. Cindy had a stable job as an administrative assistant to the building manager of a high-rise office building. She earned a steady but modest salary. Cindy enjoyed no overtime or bonus opportunity. She had relative job security, but felt unfulfilled.

Cindy's thoughts frequently drifted to her evening passion: exercise. Cindy had a thirst for exercise and worked-out at her local Life Time Fitness club for years. She was a regular at the group aerobic classes and was on a first name basis with most of the exercise trainers and staff. Trainers called her a "6er" because she exercised at Life Time Fitness six days a week. Cindy had even volunteered to lead an aerobics class if the aerobics instructor ever called in sick.

One day Cindy was talking with her daughter while playing with her grandchild. The daughter had boasted about a college friend of hers who had started her own business. The business was a tanning salon in a newly opened strip mall. The daughter raved about the freedom enjoyed by her college friend and the excitement of being her own boss. With that came abundant riches, according to the daughter. Cindy began dreaming about how she would feel if she would only find the courage to start her own business. A seed began to grow in Cindy's brain.

The seed started to germinate when Cindy was walking through a nearby strip mall that she had frequented for years. The storefront business that caught Cindy's eye was a "Hips for Women" franchise. Cindy had walked or driven by that business hundreds of times thinking only that she would never enroll at Hips for Women because it was vastly inferior to the much higher quality Life Time Fitness.

This time was different. Cindy started thinking of Hips for Women as a potential business to own and not just a place to exercise. She concentrated on what her daughter had said about her daughter's college friend opening a tanning salon. Cindy was dreaming of freedom, excitement, and profit. She walked into the store.

The Hips for Women owner greeted Cindy and started her sales pitch in hopes of enrolling Cindy into the program. Noting that Cindy was in great shape, the owner asked "where do you currently workout?" Upon hearing the answer, the owner started her spiel regarding Hips for Women's benefits over Life Time Fitness. The cost was substantially lower each month. The location was much closer to Cindy's home. Finally, the owner proudly proclaimed that the exclusivity policy prohibited any men from joining the club.

Cindy liked what she saw. She thought there could be a profitable market niche to sell exercise opportunities to women who wanted to workout in a more intimate setting without feeling the pressure of men staring at them --- judging them. Cindy understood that some women feel insecure about their body image and wanted a non-threatening environment in which to exercise.

Cindy told the owner that she wanted to explore the opportunity of owning her own Hips for Women franchise. She was given the regional franchise manager's contact information. The franchise manager met with Cindy and highlighted the benefits of franchise ownership: proven business model, franchisor training, customer name recognition, franchisor advertising support, and computerized software. The franchise manager proved to be a charismatic motivational talker. He painted a heavenly picture of franchise ownership, highlighting independence and freedom from an employer's yoke. He focused on the excitement of building a business. He caused Cindy to imagine the pride she would feel counting the profits.

The cost made Cindy mentally stagger. There was an initial $25,000 franchise fee plus an additional advertising fee of five percent of gross sales. The franchise manager also suggested that an additional $25,000 would be necessary to pay for exercise equipment, lease deposits, and leasehold furnishings and build-outs.

Cindy considered the trade-offs. She wanted to live her dream, but knew she would be losing the security of her current administrative assistant job. She had celebrated her 50th birthday and wanted her shot at success and happiness. She took the chance.

Cindy had $30,000 in her bank account and another $40,000 in her 401(k). She withdrew the $40,000 and paid the early withdrawal tax penalty to the IRS. It stung a lot, but she needed the liquidity. She incorporated her business, paid the franchise fee, and started the 7-day franchise training.

Cindy exhausted the remaining 401(k) money for the storefront lease deposit after she had located what she thought was an ideal location within a strip mall approximately eighteen miles from her home. The landlord demanded a two month deposit and required a minimum three-year term with the option of renewing for an additional three-year term. Cindy signed as president of her new corporation but had to personally guarantee the contract.

Cindy couldn't afford an attorney and believed the landlord's claim that the lease was a "standard" lease. Cindy made the fatal mistake of signing a lease that failed to include an "exclusivity" covenant that prohibited the landlord from leasing space to any other exercise-related competing businesses. Cindy was blind to the fact that she should have demanded the restrictive covenant or kept shopping.

The franchise manager was right when he estimated an additional $25,000 in leasehold build outs, exercise equipment, leasehold furnishings, computers, towels, and other business essentials. She paid the $25,000, but was left with only $5,000 in excess capital. How quickly the first $65,000 in capital expenditures vanished.

Although thinly capitalized, Cindy was ready for business. The grand opening week appeared to be a harbinger of good news to come. More than two dozen women enrolled. Proving successful was the franchise advertising coupled with the local newspaper announcements, the chamber of commerce support, and the fliers on car windshields placed throughout the business district.

The following weeks enrollment surged. Cindy strategically opened the business January 1st to take advantage of the many New

Year's resolutions to get in shape. She knew every January there was a surge in new members at her former Life Time Fitness facility.

Word spread to other exercise clubs that Cindy's Hips for Women location had a substantially lower monthly membership fee. The equipment was newer. The facility was cleaner. Momentum started to build. Women started leaving their existing clubs and women from other Hips for Women locations transferred to her club because it was located closer to their homes.

Cindy had survived the cash flow battle that every new business confronts. Revenues start at zero and begin building. But Cindy had to cover the fixed overhead from opening day no matter how much (or little) revenue came in the door. Each month, Cindy had to pay the following overhead: rent; equipment lease payments; employee wages; payroll taxes; state and federal income taxes; insurance; accounting fees; franchise fees, and advertising fees.

After six months, Cindy had hit the break-even point. The revenues generated from customer membership fees finally equaled the monthly overhead costs. However, there was nothing extra to pay Cindy a salary, nothing for profits, nothing to rebuild capital reserves, and nothing to repay the initial 401(k) investment or the initial $30,000 capital outlay. Cindy hoped the second half of the year would be better. It wasn't. Revenues stagnated. New enrollment increased about ten percent per month while existing customers left at about the same rate. Cindy fought to stay afloat until the anticipated revenue surge of the next January membership season.

The following year gave Cindy a one-two punch to the gut: a reduction in strip mall traffic combined with increased competition. Cindy's mall lost its anchor tenant, a regional food store powerhouse relocated to a newly opened mall about a half mile away. Cindy's business immediately suffered from a reduction in foot traffic thru the mall. That had been a substantial source of new customers.

The strip mall landlord landed the second punch to the gut by leasing a different vacant property to a competing workout business. Cindy was angry when she discovered the news and complained. Her landlord reviewed the lease with Cindy and noted the absence of any restrictive covenant that provided Cindy "exclusivity." Cindy was stuck.

Cindy's business started hemorrhaging cash as soon as the competitor opened its doors. The competitor began doing to Cindy what she had done to her competitors by opening Hips for Women. Cindy's customers started terminating their memberships and transferring to the newer, cleaner, and most importantly less expensive exercise club.

Cindy's cash inflow plummeted. Cindy's cash outflows remained high. The difference was paid in the short run by draining the remaining capital reserves. Cindy sought help from the franchisor in the form of additional advertising. Cindy sought help from the local banks for a business loan to afford additional advertising. Each bank declined Cindy's request because she did not have steady income from employment, she did not have a track record of consistent profitability, and she didn't have a business plan to right the sinking ship. The banks thought that any new money would be sunk with the sinking ship.

Cindy believed in herself and didn't want to give up on her dream. Cindy couldn't walk away from the most major investment of her adult life. After all, she had all of her 401(k) retirement money and her life savings invested in the business. She also had no job to fall back on. Her prior job had been filled.

So Cindy did what most small business people would do. She decided to finance the monthly loss by utilizing her personal credit cards. A thousand dollars the first month, $1,500 the next few months. Three thousand dollars and more were charged to her credit cards in future months. Additional cash flow was "created" by diverting away from the IRS employee payroll taxes withholdings and using these trust fund monies as additional business capital. Cindy knew it was wrong, but she firmly believed she could turn the business around and she would repay the diverted funds before the IRS would complain.

Employees started suspecting something was wrong when payroll checks were issued late. Employees believed Cindy the first time she said the payroll company had made an error and accepted that the checks would be late. The second time shook their confidence. Some employees quit.

The landlord was next to suspect financial problems when the first lease payment was missed. He denied Cindy's plea to apply part of the security deposit as the missed monthly rental payment. The following missed lease payment caused the landlord to issue a "5-Day Demand Notice." Cindy had five days to cure the lease default or risk the lease being terminated and the loss of her business and all leasehold improvements. Most importantly, Cindy would lose her franchise license. Her dream would be shattered.

Cindy bridged the gap with credit card advances. The employees were paid and the landlord satisfied… until next month. Cindy started taking on additional shifts, including the 6:00 a.m. to noon ship and the 6:00 p.m. to closing shift. The increase shifts allowed Cindy to reduce employee costs, but they were taking a toll on Cindy's energy and health. Ironically, the Cindy who had a passion for exercise while a member at Life Time Fitness was now too tired and exhausted to exercise… while sitting at an exercise club!

Cindy plugged along for almost two years until her credit card limit on all of her seven cards had been exhausted. No more cash advances were allowed. The minimum payments on the credit card balances did not entice the credit card providers to increase the credit limits. Cindy's attempts to obtain additional credit cards were thwarted by her ever decreasing FICO credit score. Eventually, Cindy realized there would be no more credit.

The landlord issued another "5-Day Demand Notice." Cindy couldn't cure the default and the landlord would not agree to an extension. She received and opened the landlord's attorney's letter declaring Cindy in breach of contract and the lease thereby terminated.

Cindy was crushed and tears started to flow. She now knew her business was ruined and her dreams crushed.

But in an odd way, Cindy was relieved. Relieved from the anxiety of a failing business. Relieved from the heartbreak of seeing one's dreams crumble. Relieved that she no longer had to lie to creditors --- or to herself. She wanted this chapter in her life to be over. She wanted a fresh start in life.

Cindy sought the advice of her accountant, a trusted friend and unofficial advisor. The CPA directed her to the office of an experienced bankruptcy attorney. Cindy was told about the bankruptcy powers of the automatic stay that impose a congressional injunction against all creditors attempting to collect debts against her. The creditors would be enjoined as soon as the bankruptcy case was filed.

Cindy also learned that while the business was lost forever the debts would be discharged forever too. Bankruptcy would afford her a fresh start in life. She jumped at the chance and filed Chapter 7 bankruptcy. About ninety days later Cindy had completed the bankruptcy case. She was debt free and terminated all obligations owed to the landlord, the franchisor, the equipment lessor, and most importantly the credit card companies.

Sadly, the IRS debt was not discharged because Cindy had used "trust fund money" when she had diverted employee-withheld payroll taxes away from the IRS. Cindy could live with the IRS debt as long as the other debts were discharged and eliminated for life. Bankruptcy was not what she ever thought she would do, and certainly didn't think bankruptcy was in her future when she incorporated her business. But Cindy realized that bankruptcy indeed offered her the fresh start in life that she needed.

REASON NO. 9
FAILING TO FEAR DEBT

In the early years of the 21st Century, it appeared real estate speculators could do no wrong. Home prices rocketed up and up and up. Making huge profits in real estate speculation appeared to be as easy as picking low-hanging fruit. Newly minted "real estate coaches" preached that profits were easy pickings for those resourceful enough or "smart enough" to reach-out and pick the fruit. That's where this story begins.

More than one of Hesitant Harry's friends called him a fool for not picking the juicy ripe fruit with them. Hesitant Harry still recalls the advice given by his friend Paul, a Phoenix, AZ electrical engineer with a solid steady job. "Harry, you're a fool for hesitating. The boat will sail without you. You just don't understand the new economy," Paul advised. But the market fundamentals looked confusing to Harry; so he hesitated fearing the loss of his hard earned money. Hesitant Harry was unable to pull the trigger.

Paul's "secret formula" was to purchase a piece of residential real estate without any expectation of living in the property. Paul would obtain a "no-documentation" bank loan by signing a 30-year note obligating himself to pay hundreds of thousands of dollars secured by a companion mortgage of identical amount collateralized by the property.

Paul knew he could not service the thirty-year loan on a long-term basis. But Paul believed he could handle the monthly payments from the cash flow generated by his electrical engineering job --- at least long enough to flip the home for a profit. Then the sale proceeds would be applied first to closing costs, next to realtor fees, then to pay off the bank's note and mortgage, with the remaining monies kept in Paul's pocket as profit.

Harry hesitated again while Paul bought his next investment property by employing his secret formula. Paul sold it for a large profit. Paul repeatedly shared his secret formula with Harry to entice him to join Paul on the next big speculative adventure. Notwithstanding, Harry hesitated again---now with doubts creeping into his mind as to whether Harry was crazy, or was it Paul. After all, the profits reaped by Paul appeared to be buttressing Paul's secret strategy.

Paul used some of his substantial profits from the sale to host a celebration to rejoice over his sharing in the "new economy" largesse. At the celebration party, Paul announced for all celebrants to hear, "Hey Harry, remember I offered you this great opportunity first, but I guessed you just can't teach a bankruptcy lawyer like Harry new tricks…maybe next time." The celebrants laughed along with Paul at Harry's expense. Hesitant Harry congratulated Paul for his success, but still didn't understand how Paul's success could continue.

So Harry continued to hesitate and was unable to pull the investment trigger on Paul's next big adventure. Hesitant Harry's legal and CPA training made his Spiderman senses tingle. Harry knew Paul and many investors like Paul had obtained mortgage debts far greater than they could ever pay. But mortgage brokers didn't appear to care that the loans could not be serviced long-term. Some mortgage brokers didn't even care that the investor's income was inaccurately reported. Investors didn't care either that they couldn't service the loans since the goal was to own the investment property only long enough to "flip" the house for a large profit.

How long could this continue? Hesitant Harry began asking all the right questions. When did average Americans start believing they were qualified to speculate in real estate? Who trained them in real estate fundamentals? Where did they study the intricacies of real estate financing and its legal consequences? How did they acquire their real estate expertise? What prior real estate experience did they have before taking the greatest financial gamble of their lives? Why did Americans disregard the risks and believe only vast profits lay ahead of them?

Suddenly, Hesitant Harry had an epiphany one day while sitting in the bankruptcy courtroom waiting for his next court hearing. **The fear of debt has died**. The fear of being homeless and penniless that had stalked the Great Depression generation has disappeared. Perhaps it is because of the ever present government support system and its safety net. The 21st Century speculative investors have never felt and cannot imagine the economic devastation endured by the Great Depression generation.

Paul and other speculative investors were totally discounting the financial and legal ramifications of loading up on debt. They knew they had no ability to service the long-term debt. But debt was not their problem they reasoned. There were no worries or fears of too much debt. Instead, Paul and his fellow speculators began to believe the more debt the better. Debt was seen as "leverage." Debt translated into opportunities to make even more money.

Hesitant Harry's father was a wise and profound man who was both a lawyer in his earlier career and later a highly respected state court judge. After years and years on the judicial bench, he shared a pearl of wisdom with Harry. He said, "Son, fear debt like a man fears death. Keep a close eye on it so it doesn't creep up on you. And never unnecessarily put your neck in the financial hangman's noose."

Regrettably, Paul never met Hesitant Harry's father before Paul's final speculative investment --- which started Paul down the road to bankruptcy. Paul never feared that an investment could sour, really sour. After all, all boats rise at high tide and investment property only moves in one direction: UP, UP, UP.

Paul never thought about the legal consequences IF real estate prices decreased. That was "Old Economy thinking, not New Economy reality," Paul said to himself. Paul never considered engaging an attorney to create a limited liability company so the investment property could be titled in the LLC's name. Paul didn't acknowledge the danger of obligating himself to a multi-million dollar loan.

So, Hesitant Harry's electrical engineer friend, decided to invest in the "big leagues" to make a "big score." Paul lived in Phoenix and had very little knowledge of Florida real estate other than what he learned when he was on vacation. Research was not his thing. Paul liked to trust his instincts.

Paul learned of a no-miss opportunity from one of his golfing buddies at his private country club. Some of his golf club members were investing in a spectacular new condominium development being built in tropical Naples, Florida. The goal was to flip the condos before the development was completed.

Paul smelled big profits and wanted in on the deal. Paul purchased four separate condominiums in the Naples condo development at the price of $1,000,000 each for a total of $4 million. Paul utilized the $400,000 profits from his prior real estate investments as the down-payment for the Big Kill. A $100,00 own-payment was applied to each of the four condos.

At the closing, Paul executed four separate no-documentation thirty-year notes for $900,000 each for a total of $3.6 million of secured mortgage debt. Paul never considered living in the condos or leasing the condos to generate cash to service the debt. Instead, Paul's intention was to "flip" the condo's for big profit by selling each condo for at least $1.3 million and pocketing a cool $300,000 profit for each condo for a total profit of $1.2 million for only a couple months of work.

Then it happened. The real estate market started collapsing! At first, Paul tried to deny that the market was collapsing. He held onto the condo properties thinking that the market would rebound despite a fellow investor selling his condo investment for a $50,000 loss.

Eventually, he realized his mistake as the economic downturn deepened. First, he tried to sell each condo at $1,000,000 just to break-even, but he couldn't. Months later Paul dropped the listing price to $800,000 each. Still no takers. The market price was falling faster than Paul was reducing his asking price.

Six months later, and one realtor later, the price was reduced again to $599,999. The market was as dead as a doornail since the economy had worsened and the market had been flooded with other properties being sold by panicking investors.

Paul was stuck. The mortgage lender started calling and pressuring Paul. Paul couldn't believe this nightmare was happening to him. Screaming at the new Florida realtor to find a buyer became a semi-weekly affair. The realtor eventually had enough abuse and severed the relationship. The listing agreement was severed and another engaged. The new realtor listed the condos for $299,000 each.

Eventually, Paul found a buyer who agreed to pay $299,999 for each condo and started to negotiate a "short-sale" with the bank. Paul found it a bitter pill to swallow that he would be losing $701,00 n each condo for a total loss of approximately $2.8 million plus the cost of the realtor fees and property taxes.

But the short-sale fell through when the new buyer could not obtain financing and the mortgage lender refused to "forgive" Paul from his financial obligation to pay the mortgage deficiency, that is the difference between the amount of the mortgage debt owed to the lender and the proceeds paid to the lender at the sale. After all, the mortgage lender was not a charity.

Paul knew there wouldn't be any celebration party after this speculative adventure. Paul was stuck owing $4,000,000 in secured mortgage debt with monthly payment obligations radically beyond anything he could service from his salary as an electrical engineer. After swallowing the bitter pill, Paul called Hesitant Harry to speak confidentially about his bankruptcy options. Paul learned the benefits of filing Chapter 7 bankruptcy. Paul needed to get his head out of the hangman's noose. Paul needed a fresh start in life.

Paul ultimately filed bankruptcy and obtained a full bankruptcy discharged of his debts. Paul simply surrendered his interest in the condo development and shed the $4,000,000 mortgage obligations as part of the bankruptcy process. Shortly thereafter, Paul shared his misfortune with his neighbor one day during a backyard barbeque. Paul's neighbor was shocked and just couldn't believe that bankruptcy could ever have happened to an upper-middle class electrical engineer with a good, stable job. But it did.

REASON NO. 10
SELF-LAWYERING

Tom and Brenda were solid middle to upper-middle class people enjoying life fully while raising a family in the suburbs. They were proud parents of three children ages four, seven, and eleven. Brenda was pregnant with their fourth child and enjoyed her role as the stay-at-home mom who loved and nurtured the children. Tom had a strong, stable job as a regional manager of a national retail computer store.

Tom was great at his job and enjoyed promotion after promotion. Their family income was more than they needed; trappings of solid upper-middle class life were numerous and vacations plentiful. Tom drove a gently-used black E320 Mercedes to his local country club and Brenda drove a new blue 5-Series BMW.

Neighbors looking at the happy family would never guess that Tom and Brenda had just made the worse financial mistake of their life. A mistake so simple, yet so financially catastrophic that it would result in them losing their home and having to file bankruptcy.

Specifically, Tom and Brenda had just executed a real estate contract to buy their new dream home which waived the seemingly innocuous protective contingency clause that would have allowed them to void the dream home contract if they were unable to sell their current home.

Tom and Brenda had been in the market for awhile to buy their dream home. They then currently owned a $325,000 three-bedroom home in a wonderful family-oriented community with solid schools. But they wanted to buy a larger home because of the fourth child soon to be born. Brenda would peruse the real estate section of the weekly local paper looking for the latest open houses and worked diligently with the realtor to identify houses for sale in Tom and Brenda's price range.

Many weekends were spent touring the plethora of magnificent homes at their new price range of $600,000. Tom's income had increased substantially since they purchased their current $325,000 home and they knew they could afford monthly payments on their $600,000 dream home.

One weekend it happened! The realtor called Brenda and announced that the home of their dreams was just listed in the multiple listing service. Brenda jumped on the lead. Brenda and the realtor drove-by the home that very day. Although they only saw the outside of the home, Brenda knew it was her dream home where her children would be raised and family memories made.

Tom and Brenda received a tour of the house that weekend with their children in tow. The house took Tom's breath away. It was everything he had dreamed about: a center entrance, red brick Georgian, a three-car garage, and a spacious yard. Their dream home had a cherry wood paneled office for Tom to do his evening and weekend paperwork. The kitchen had beautiful maple wood cabinetry with a granite topped center island, perfect for cooking and entertaining.

A family room with a 20-foot cathedral ceiling attached to the east end of the kitchen with only a railing and pillars to demark the beginning of the family room. Tom's head danced with visions of watching football and basketball games on the wall-mounted 70-inch big screen television.

Brenda's mind flooded with images of the kids playing as she supervised while busy preparing meals in the kitchen. Tom and Brenda were hooked once they saw the vast master bedroom with the tray ceiling and ceramic tiled master bathroom with the Jacuzzi tub. They were urged by the realtor to buy the house before anyone else could "steal" it.

The realtor drove Tom and Brenda to the realtor's office to prepare a written offer to purchase the dream home. They all agreed $600,000 would be a great price, believing that the sellers could get even more. The realtor prepared the offer and tendered it to Tom and Brenda for signing. Brenda signed immediately. Tom paused to read the fine print on page five of the contract. Tom asked several questions to clarify the meaning of the complicated contract. His worries were alleviated on all issues but one: the waiving of the contingency that allowed Tom and Brenda to void the dream home contact if they failed to sell their then current home.

The realtor understood Tom's objection and sensed the potential loss of the $30,000 real estate commission that would be shared with the listing agency. The realtor began explaining that the form real estate contract could be trusted because it had been drafted and approved by both the local realtor board and the local bar association real estate committee. This form contract originally provided Tom and Brenda with a protective contingency provision that would have allowed them to void the real estate contract to purchase the new dream home if Tom and Brenda were unable to sell their then current home.

Nevertheless, the realtor strongly urged Tom and Brenda to waive the protective contingency provision "for their own good." Playing on Brenda's fear of losing the opportunity to buy the dream home, the realtor suggested that the seller of the home would most likely reject Tom and Brenda's contract offer if the contingency provision was not waived. Then the dream home seller could sell the home to someone else. Brenda's objection collapsed, but Tom was still unsure.

"What if I am unable to sell my current home? How could I afford to pay the mortgages on both the current home and the new dream home?" Tom asked. Tom expressed a healthy dose of old-fashioned fear; the fear of not being able to pay the mortgage. "Don't worry. Your house will sell in forty-five days, ninety days at the latest," said the realtor. Homes appeared to be selling, but Tom had started to wonder why there was such a large and growing selection of homes in the $600,000 price range from which to choose. Was it possible the housing market was cooling?

After a long pause, and a deep breath, Tom looked at Brenda and said "let's do it!" They signed the papers and waived the protective contingency provision that would have allowed them to void the contract if Tom and Brenda could not sell their existing home--- waiving the very shield that would have protected them from the need to file bankruptcy.

Tom and Brenda closed on the dream house about ninety days later, signing a $570,000 mortgage after making a five percent down-payment. Tom knew he could afford the $5,200 monthly mortgage payments, but only if Tom didn't have to pay the $3,400 monthly mortgage payments on the original home along with the real estate taxes and insurance, which were not escrowed in the mortgage payment and had to be paid separately. They had no choice. The original home mortgage payments along with taxes and insurance had to be paid from the family's savings account.

Tom and Brenda were thrilled about moving into their new dream home. At first, the $3,400 mortgage payment on the original home didn't hurt too much. Tom had budgeted $10,000 of his savings to be drained by carrying the original home mortgage payments. Three months later, the entire $10,000 savings had been exhausted and still no offers on the original home.

The second installment of the annual real estate taxes came due and Tom had to pay another $4,000 to the local county treasurer. Three more months expired along with the end of Milwaukee's traditional spring-summer selling season. Tom had now spent almost $25,000 to carry the original home.

Tom began to worry now that the selling season had ended. Tom knew that few homes in Milwaukee sold after the children began their school year in September. Most families in Milwaukee simply do not want to separate their children from their schools during the school year. That meant Tom and Brenda would have to carry their prior home through the fall and long winter with hopes of selling the next spring season. That also meant Tom would have to pay nine more mortgage payments, or a total of $30,600 plus utility bills, taxes, and insurance.

Tom knew he couldn't afford the $30,600 on top of the $25,000 he had already paid. So he instructed his realtor to drop the listing price on the original home. The price was dropped to an amount equal to the mortgage owed plus any realtor fees that would be charged on the sales transaction. Still no buyers. Tom couldn't drop the price any lower to attract "bargain shoppers" because the amount of sales proceeds at a reduced price wouldn't generate enough money at the closing table to pay off the mortgage lender who had encumbered the subject property with a consensual mortgage lien.

Tom felt trapped and knew he would be forced to pay the mortgage until the spring season where a higher price could be obtained. Tom also knew that he was on the verge of exhausting his savings at the very time his wife Brenda wanted to spend substantial sums decorating and furnishing their new dream home.

Tom and Brenda's financial world was shattering but they were locked into long-term secured debt. The car payments were monthly obligations that would last for at least five more years. But the mortgage payments were monthly obligations that would last for twenty-five to thirty years.

Tom and Brenda decided they had to withdraw their small nest-egg nestled securely in Tom's IR ualified 401(k) retirement account. They knew the IRS would charge a substantial penalty for early withdrawal, but they needed the money. Tom used the 401(k) money to help pay the nearly $8,600 in combined monthly mortgage payments and $1,050 combined car payments. Tom understood that his income from his job as a regional manager of a national retail computer store was strong, but he inherently understood that it was vastly insufficient to pay the $9,650 in combined mortgages and car payments while also maintaining the county club membership and other trappings of upper middle-class life.

So, Tom and Brenda focused their attention on slashing discretionary spending. Without question, the country club was the first luxury to hit the chopping block. Tom thought about selling the luxury vehicles, but realized that he was in a negative equity position--the fair market value of the vehicles had reduced to a value that was less than the payoff balance owed on the vehicles. Hence, the surrender of the vehicles would cost Tom and Brenda money and they couldn't afford to buy replacement vehicles consistent with their "station in life."

The oldest child was pulled from the traveling soccer team to save money. Music lessons were cancelled. Ballet training was terminated. Brenda did her part by tightening the food budget and restricting clothing consumption to just the essentials. New furniture, new drapes, and new wall paper were definitely out. Tom and Brenda could not afford to entertain.

The winter ended with Tom and Brenda in a precarious financial position. Their savings had been exhausted and Tom's qualified 401(k) drained. The once-affluent family had had to rely on credit card debt to "make ends meet" since Tom's take-home pay was insufficient to pay the monthly bills.

Summer sun finally started shining on Milwaukee again, but the housing market hadn't blossomed as the realtor had anticipated. The housing market had hit a slump and prices had decreased sharply from the prior summer. Tom and Brenda's dream of selling their original home had been crushed. The realtor offered encouraging words suggesting that the housing prices may increase by the end of the summer. But Tom suspected that the pressure on housing prices to decline would not be soon abated.

Tom didn't believe the realtor, but had no options. The empty original house stayed on the market at the lowest price possible to pay off the mortgage and realtor commission. But the fair market price of similar homes on the market were far less than Tom and Brenda's asking price. Summer came and went with the house still on the market. Tom stopped paying the mortgage on the original home when he reached the maximum credit available on this credit cards.

Several months later, Tom received a "notice of default" letter from his mortgage lender stating that the lender would be filing foreclosure if the mortgage default was not cured. Tom called the bank and explained his predicament. The bank's legal department representative was sympathetic to Tom's plight, but still demanded that Tom cure the mortgage default or the bank would foreclose. About two months later, a Milwaukee County sheriff's deputy appeared at Brenda's door to serve them with the Summons and Complaint to Foreclose Real Estate. Brenda was in a panic and called Tom immediately at work.

At that point, Tom knew hope was lost. More than a year had expired since the purchase of their dream home with combined monthly mortgage payments on both homes during that year exceeding $115,000. All savings and retirement funds had been drained. Credit card balances were spiraling up every month. The financial strain was causing Tom and Brenda to fight over issues that had never caused an argument when money was plentiful and debts were minimal. The financial stress caused Tom to be less attentive to demands of his job. His job performance suffered and threatened his job security.

Despite enjoying a great job with a great salary, Tom began talking to Brenda about filing bankruptcy. Initially Brenda resisted the idea. Tom felt embarrassed, but trapped. He could see no way out of the financial trap. "If only we had not bought the dream home," said Brenda.

Tom whispered under his breath, "If only we had not waived the protective contingency provision allowing me to void the contract if we could not sell our original home." Tom learned the hard lesson of why those real estate contingency protections have been afforded to home buyers for generations. Tom also then realized why those protections shouldn't be casually discarded during a time of home buying euphoria.

So Tom and Brenda sought bankruptcy advice from a skilled Milwaukee-based bankruptcy attorney who had been practicing law more than twenty-five years. They learned that bankruptcy law would automatically enjoin the bank from proceeding with the foreclosure proceeding. Credit card collectors would be prohibited from calling. Creditors could NOT garnish any wages, file any lawsuit, lien any assets, or levy any bank accounts. Plus, Tom and Brenda would be allowed to retain their dream home and peacefully surrender their interest in the original home. The mortgage obligations associated with the original home mortgage would terminate.

Tom and Brenda filed for Chapter 13 bankruptcy protection. They terminated their mortgage obligation on their original home, discharged ninety percent of their credit card debts, and established a repayment plan to repay the mortgage arrearage on their dream home that had previously been in default. Bankruptcy allowed them to save their dream home and proved to be the solution to their problems by vanquishing the financial demons in their lives.

ABOUT THE AUTHOR

Attorney Robert Schaller has practiced law for more than twenty-seven years and has helped clients discharge or restructure approximately half a billion dollars in debts.

Each day he provides bankruptcy relief to individuals seeking protection from creditors. Attorney Schaller has filed thousands of bankruptcy cases, helping individuals and families obtain a fresh start in life by shedding the yoke of unmanageable debt.

Schaller is licensed to practice before the U.S. Supreme Court and the Illinois Supreme Court. He is the president of the National Bankruptcy Academy. Plus, Schaller is a member of the American Bankruptcy Institute and the National Association of Consumer Bankruptcy Attorneys.

Schaller has served on the editorial board and/or editor-in-chief for a number of legal journals, including the Chicago Bar Association's CBA Record, Chicago Bar Association's Young Lawyers Journal, and the DuPage County Bar Association's The Brief. He has published numerous journal articles and two law review articles, one each in both the DePaul Law Review and the Chicago-Kent Law Review.

He received his B.S. in Accountancy in 1982 from the University of Illinois in Champaign-Urbana, Illinois. He earned his J.D. from DePaul University College of Law in 1985 and served on the College's law review. His M.B.A. studies matriculated at the University of Chicago in 1986. Schaller is also a Certified Public Accountant.

Attorney Schaller is the founder of the Schaller Law Firm, P.C. and concentrates his legal practice on clients residing in Illinois. Schaller lives in Hinsdale, Illinois with his wife Nancy and daughters, Katie and Beth.

CPSIA information can be obtained at www.ICGtesting.com
Printed in the USA
LVOW08*0459301113

363122LV00001B/1/P